SECOND EDITION

LIVESTOCK
PROTECTION DOGS

Selection, Care and Training

Orysia Dawydiak
David E. Sims

Library of Congress Cataloging-in-Publication Data

Dawydiak, Orysia, 1952-
    Livestock protection dogs : selection, care, and training / Orysia Dawydiak
       and David E. Sims.-- 2nd ed.
      p. cm.
    Sims's name appears first on the earlier edition.
    Includes bibliographical references and index.
    ISBN 1-57779-062-6
    1. Livestock protection dogs. I. Sims, David E., 1950- II. Title.

SF428.6.S56 2003
636.737--dc22   2003063705

The information contained in this book is complete and accurate to the best of our knowledge. All recommendations are made without guarantee on the part of the author or Alpine Publications, Inc. The author and publisher disclaim any liability with the use of this information.

This book is available at special quantity discounts for breeders and for club promotions, premiums, or educational use. Write for details.

For the sake of simplicity, the terms "he" or "she" are sometimes used to identify an animal or person. These are used in the generic sense only. No discrimination of any kind is intended toward either sex.

Many manufacturers secure trademark rights for their products. When Alpine Publications is aware of a trademark claim, we identify the product name by using initial capital letters.

Cover Design: Laura Newport
Cover Photo: (top) David E. Sims; (bottom) Agostino Molinelli.
Editing: Deborah Helmers
Photographs: All photographs by the author unless otherwise indicated.

Printed in the United States of America.

Contents

To our parents, Marion Sims, and Walter
and Olga Dawydiak

Preface to the Second Edition

This edition of Livestock Protection Dogs offers many new photographs, and some of the best from the first edition. Readers of the first edition spoke well of our "quiz photos," so we've added more of them. Training methods have been refined, notably with heavier emphasis on rewarding correct behavior instead of punishing inappropriate actions (negative reinforcement does have an important role, however). The range of animals that livestock protection dogs may protect is increasing, so a new chapter on unusual livestock has been written (not that llamas seem so unusual anymore).

With the growth in popularity of livestock protection dogs, there are more breeders. A chapter has been added to advise potential breeders on the rewards and headaches that lie ahead. Breeding two dogs is easy. Successful, long-term breeding is a challenging combination of applied psychology, art and science that we cannot specifically define, but can allude to. Most would-be dog breeders burn out after one or two litters. We hope we can help to allieviate this situation by helping breeders be better prepared and make better decisions.

Our societies are increasingly urban. The separation of town dweller from farmer, previously no more than one or two generations removed, is now on its way to being complete. City dwellers no longer know how animals are kept in agriculture, and don't care to empathize with the needs of farmers and ranchers. Livestock protection doesn't get singled out in this separation; it is but one more example. Dogs that look gorgeous and have been selected to work in an agricultural setting are being acquired as pets, and the demands for a domestic pet are being brought to bear on breeders. In fact, some livestock protection dog breeds have been used in home and show for so long that there are now sub-types of the breeds, for companion or for farm work.

We were astounded one day when a message we posted on a livestock protection dog list that we thought was an innocuous piece of training advice was blasted by a breeder we had not met. This breeder offered the opinion that she would never expose her dogs to harsh weather conditions or the danger of predators. "Her" dogs would only be sold to good suburban homes, and those of us who actually put dogs in danger of attack from other canids were being cruel. Shortly after, another breeder offered the same opinion and suggested that in North America the time had come to stop using these dogs to protect livestock. She was of the opinion that livestock protection dogs belonged exclusively in the show ring and in safe homes.

Livestock protection dogs have indeed been killed while defending livestock. They have been outnumbered by wolves or coyotes, and overpowered by bears and cougars. We do not refer to fatal incidents to glorify death or fighting. However, these magnificent breeds have been selected for millennia to protect. To deny a livestock protection dog the opportunity to be a part of an extended pack or grouping is the mental equivalent to chaining that dog alone in the backyard. While fatalities rarely happen, and most protection work is accomplished with barks, growls and posturing, we should acknowledge and celebrate that our livestock protection dogs are willing, if needed, to give their lives in protection of their charges. Is this a heritage we want to dilute or remove from these breeds? (By our estimates, work-related fatalities are less common than urban hit-by-car deaths.)

Meanwhile, increasing numbers of urbanites are electing to move out of the city and live on small rural properties. Obtaining a flock of birds or sheep is a life-long dream that has finally been realized. Small-time property owners, farmers and ranchers continue to need good working dogs. Despite the ready availability of facts in this age of electronic communication, there remains a niche for a book as a single source of advice on a most noble lineage of working dogs, to openly acknowledge the problems they may bring with them at an individual level and in a more global or political context, and to offer training tips that have been previously learned through the slow and sometimes painful methods of trial and error.

We hope you will enjoy your experience of owning or raising a livestock protection dog and request that you will, as others have before you, share any unusual experiences with us to enrich future editions of this book.

Maremma pup bonding with sheep at the Hampshire College Livestock Dog Project barn. Photo by Lorna Coppinger.

Preface to the Original Edition

This text is designed to aid people who are interested in, or who have decided to invest in and train, a livestock protection dog. We begin with four assumptions about serious livestock protection dog owners. First, we shall assume that you are aware that no two dogs will behave in an identical manner. Indeed, there is probably as much personality variability within the breeds of livestock protection dogs as there is between them. Therefore you must be flexible in your interpretation of our advice.

Second, we will assume that you have some basic knowledge of canine behavior and psychology. Training a protection dog without any prior experience with dogs will be more difficult, but not impossible. Community libraries contain texts on fundamentals of dog behavior and training. We suggest that you should be able to train a dog to stay, sit and come before attempting to train a livestock protection dog. We offer this recommendation because livestock guard dogs should not be taken to dog obedience schools. Their effectiveness may be diminished if they become overly socialized to other canines.

Third, and perhaps most important, we shall assume that you are firmly committed to making the most of a substantial investment. This commitment includes a willingness to care for the dog's physical and mental soundness, and to attend to problems of behavior as soon as they occur, not days or weeks later. Our assumptions are that you are prepared to build or modify fencing or gates or feeding areas if a need for these changes becomes apparent.

Fourth, while you may choose to invest in a livestock protection dog mainly for financial reasons, you should also just plain like dogs. Livestock protection dogs are only one of many management techniques available for control of predation problems. They probably will not work well for a person who is inherently indifferent, or unfriendly, towards dogs.

If these are reasonable assumptions on our part, we are willing to do our best to help you train a livestock protection dog. You are undertaking a noble challenge, one that will reward you for years.

As this book is being published, widespread use of livestock protection dogs has yet to enter its second decade. Puppy aptitude testing is still in its infancy. Some of the thoughts presented within this book may be out of date within several years. Readers are encouraged to correspond with the authors to ensure that future editions include as many successful training methods as possible. Your responses to this book would be most appreciated.

Photo by Ray Coppinger.

Acknowledgments

The writing of this book has been a team effort. Individual photographers are recognized in the photo captions, but for those whose photos are not included, thanks to you as well for taking the time and effort to send photos to us. Dr. Caroline Runyon, veterinary orthopedic surgeon, provided the examples of healthy and dysplastic hips which are shown in the chapter on health issues. Shelley Ebbett, medical photographer, took the photos of the hips for us.

Jennifer Brown, Marsha Peterson and Diane Spisak read and critiqued various drafts of this edition, offering many constructive suggestions. Within the clubs that represent livestock protection breeds are many people who have toiled on behalf of their breeds to present responsible information to the public, to rescue neglected animals, and to advance our understanding of these magnificent dogs. While unnamed in this book, their efforts made the factual compilation of breed information possible.

We thank the livestock protection dog owners who have shared with us over the years the little tidbits of information, the training tips, the motivators, the ways to use positive instead of negative reinforcement, which collectively add up to wisdom. Without such team effort, this book could not be written. The editorial team at Alpine Publications has done a wonderful job preparing out manuscript for publication. For their professional, constructive suggestions, we thank them.

A mature Akbash Dog lives with and guards goats in Oregon. Blackberry bushes are abundant in the Willamette Valley. Goats are an ecological way to control their spread. The farm is visited regularly by coyotes, wolves and dog packs, yet suffers few losses of livestock due to a management system that includes several livestock protection dogs. Photo by David E. Sims.

What is a
Livestock
Protection Dog ?

CHAPTER

1

In Old World countries where livestock protection dogs have been traditionally used, lifestyles and farming practices are different than those we know in North America. Throughout Asia, the Middle East and the Mediterranean Basin, full-time shepherds are common. Sheep owners in a village often form communal flocks of sheep during the summer months when high country pastures can be used for grazing. Shepherds and livestock protection dogs accompany large bands of sheep to mountain meadows. During these times when many protection dogs are present, older dogs help to discipline and train younger ones. With one or more shepherds always on duty, undesirable behaviors can be spotted and corrected immediately. In this setting many stimuli act on a protection dog, including social interactions with other dogs. Boredom is unlikely to

Working Maremmas in rural Italy with Sirio Di Michele, a noted breeder of working dogs. Photo by Agostino Molinelli.

1

Turkish shepherd with Kangal Dogs accompanying flock out of village in Sivas province. Photo by Sue Kocher.

occur. If attacked or threatened by a predator, a protection dog can reasonably expect to be backed up by his fellow pack members. He can also expect that a shepherd will be somewhere nearby, if not always in sight. In all, a rather non-mechanized, leisurely environment exists in which protection dogs coexist with humans and livestock, to their collective benefit.

Most North American farms would not fit into the scenario described above. Farms here have fenced pastures in lieu of open mountain rangelands. Livestock are moved abruptly from pasture to pasture, sometimes by truck. There are few full-time shepherds, goat herders, or cattle tenders. Protection dogs are often required to work alone without aid or training from an experienced pack of peer dogs. Many protection dogs are initially placed with livestock that have learned to fear dogs. A significant part of the task of protection is having the confidence of the animals to be guarded. North American guard dogs may be expected to develop their self-confidence with livestock that will run away from them or even show hostility. After a protection dog has gained the confidence of the flock or herd and has matured into a successful guardian, he is almost always left alone to perform what can be a very boring duty.

When such factors are considered, you may wonder why protection dogs transplanted from the tranquil mountains of Europe and Asia are able to work at all in the United States and Canada. Yet they do! The reason for their success is not so much the training techniques that are described in the succeeding chapters, but rather the highly evolved instincts of the dogs. If you have purchased a healthy protection breed puppy with an established guarding pedigree, he will probably become a good livestock guardian, in spite of any errors you, the owner/trainer, might commit. In fact, you will never actually "train" your protection dog to protect. You will instead attempt to create an environment in which the dog is able to develop and express his inherited talents.

WHAT DOES A GOOD LIVESTOCK PROTECTION DOG DO?

A mature, confident livestock protection dog is rarely out of sight or hearing of his flock. ("Sheep" and "flock" will be used frequently in this text, because most readers will be interested in the use of protection dogs for sheep operations. However, these words are not used to exclude other livestock; protection dogs perform very well in defense of cattle, goats, horses, poultry, equipment, and even human families.) The protection dog is a calm animal that moves slowly to avoid disturbing the livestock. We have observed protection dogs walk carefully around, rather than near or between, ewes with newborn lambs, as if to avoid interfering with the lamb-ewe bonding. They appear to sense a different attitude from these ewes, who change their behavior when they have newborn lambs near them. A good protection dog possesses better than average senses of hearing, sight and smell. He will often become curious and defensive whenever something out of the ordinary occurs.

The following example illustrates some of these traits. When we were living in Oregon, during the winter months a neighbor regularly filled a hay manger for his cattle at around 6:00 A.M. His manger was near the edge of two of our fields, where we kept sheep and protection dogs. The dogs watched him arrive and perform his chores. Occasionally they barked, but usually they just watched and his activities became part of their regular routine. One day, the neighbor sent a hired hand in his place. The assistant performed the chores in a different manner and had a distinctive voice. His mannerisms made the cattle nervous and upset the routine for our dogs. The protection dogs in the fields did nothing more than bark during this incident. However, a bitch happened to be nursing a litter at the time, and had stronger than usual protection instincts. (Protecting, unlike the aggressive form of police dog work or livestock herding, is an extension of maternal and paternal instincts. Livestock protection dogs protect objects that have been included in their "family" of possessions. Since our bitch had a litter with her at the time, she was more protective than usual.) Upon hearing the sounds of the upset cattle, the hired hand and the barking of the other dogs, she rushed out to the fence separating our properties. She found a weak spot in the fence and charged through, forcing the man to remain in his truck until the bitch finally left. Our neighbor reported the incident to us later that week, more amused than concerned. We repaired the fence and moved the bitch to another area—our neighbor moved his manger farther from our fence line.

Several lessons may be elicited from this incident. First, the dogs were responding to an upset in their routine. A good protection dog loves an orderly, predictable world. Second, a responsible dog owner will have to be considerate of his neighbors, usually by ensuring that the dogs remain on their owner's property. Third, dogs may choose to "protect" objects, livestock or territory that the owner does not have in mind. Our dogs had chosen to include the nearby cattle as part of their "domain" (although another bitch subsequently chose to stand between the neighbors' cattle and our new lamb crop, as if to protect the lambs from the curious cattle). Our dogs exercised their protective instincts without regard for human constraints such as property lines or fences. This tendency can be heartwarming and useful, but can also be a problem if neighbors do not appreciate the dogs' actions.

Thus far, a good livestock protection dog has been defined as one that is calm, loves order, is healthy, protective and sensitive to the moods of the livestock, and possesses superior senses of sight, smell and hearing. Are there any other desirable traits? Most people do not want an overprotective dog that will bite any stranger entering the field—a sociability factor must be considered. A dog that does not eat too much food is also an economic benefit. This is a rather subjective consideration, but fits in well with the need for a calm animal. Calm animals often have lower rates of metabolism—they eat less and expend less energy.

The good livestock protection dog will look forward to interactions with his master, but will not be too fawning or dependent on the master for love and affection. In other words, a good protection dog will be self-confident and capable of making independent decisions. Many dog breeds today seem to exist only to please their masters. These breeds are not very likely to be good livestock protection dogs.

The independent nature of livestock protection breeds can be illustrated by an anecdote from central Turkey. An elderly shepherd died while pasturing his flock in the high mountains one summer. When the shepherd and his flock did not return to the village that fall, other shepherds went up to search for him. They found the flock safely grazing in the highlands, accompanied by the dogs and a litter of pups. The dogs had managed to feed themselves by hunting for small game, while guarding the flock and training the younger dogs. This demonstrates not only the independence and trustworthiness of these dogs, but the strong survival instincts they possess.

The ideal protection dog will react toward strange humans in the manner desired by the master. Some situations will call for a decidedly unfriendly response to strangers. In most cases, though, the owner will want his dog to be neutral or friendly toward other people. The way a dog responds to strange humans is primarily determined by the owner, although there is also a genetic component to a dog's temperament. This is one aspect of the dog's behavior that can be influenced more by training than by instinct.

There is one other factor that should be considered. In the hierarchy of canine dominance, large size is usually desirable. A larger dog will usually enjoy a higher position in the pecking order. Therefore, large protection dogs will probably be challenged less often by marauding dogs, wolves or coyotes. This is not to say that the largest breed of protection dog is necessarily the best, or the largest dog in a pack will be the most dominant. Size is just one more variable to be considered. On the other hand, larger protection dogs have been known to give owners a more difficult time. A handler's size and ability to command respect from the dog will affect the development of a bond between dog and owner. Larger dogs—and these tend to be males—are more likely to challenge the authority of their owners. Smaller, gentler owners may back away the first time a 100-pound youngster challenges authority. Therefore, even if a larger dog will tend to have less trouble with predators, the control factor may, in some situations, be more important. Larger dogs are not always best.

We have discussed the qualities that predispose a good guardian. A dog possessing these traits will probably develop a protection routine of his own. He may regularly patrol his domain. Most males and many females mark their territorial perimeter with urine, which acts as a chemical message to other canids that the area is off limits. Although the

Slovakian Cuvac pup in training. Photo by Robin Rigg.

dog may occasionally sleep with the livestock, more usually he will remain a short distance from them. The dog will, with experience, learn which upsets of the routine are significant and which can be ignored. He will spend a lot of time resting near the livestock or slowly patrolling the pasture. Many protection dogs will display nocturnal behavior, patrolling more actively at night than during the day. Companion dog owners may find this a problem if their dog is left outdoors and barks at night.

There have been reports of protection dogs herding livestock. In many of these situations, coyotes or dog packs were either in the field or in the vicinity. Some protection dogs may herd livestock together at night or in times of danger but will otherwise leave them alone. These are, however, exceptional instances. Livestock protection dogs are not herding dogs in the usual sense of the phrase and would not be good candidates for herding dog training. Certain breeds show an inclination to herd under the direction of a shepherd (see Chapter Two); however, the style is completely different from typical herding dogs such as Border Collies.

WHAT NOT TO EXPECT
FROM A LIVESTOCK PROTECTION DOG

You may hear of someone's dog staying with the children all day, then leaving at night to protect the livestock. There have also been instances of

Akbash Dogs with their flock on Prince Edward Island. Notice the cropped ears on the male, Asil Akkush, who was imported from Turkey. Photo by Orysia Dawydiak.

protection dogs routinely hopping fences to patrol several pastures of goats and sheep, some of the pastures being miles from others. These, however, are examples of exceptional protective behavior. To expect this type of behavior from every dog would be unreasonable. More often than not, the exceptional dogs are owned by experienced dog handlers who have a good grasp of canine psychology. They can influence a dog in ways that develop his fullest potential. Most first-time owners will not be able to do that. For example, most protection dogs will not be able to act as family dogs part of the time and livestock protection dogs the rest of the time. People are much more fun to be with than livestock. Especially when young, a dog that is given the choice of living with either people or livestock will usually choose to remain full-time with humans.

Some people would like to have a dog that could be moved between flocks and pastures, and perhaps even between owners, yet work consistently in all situations. This has been done, but once again it is the exception, not the norm. If this is to be expected of a mature guardian, there are certain ways in which the puppy should be handled early on to adapt him to this lifestyle. Similarly, a farm dog that for five years has only known his band of 60 sheep and well-fenced 115 acres may not subsequently work optimally on open range covering thousands of acres.

Do not expect a protection dog to be independent most of the time, yet completely submissive and obedient at the whim of the master. Independence and submissiveness are not totally compatible traits. A protection dog does not need to know complex obedience commands that require hours of practice and repetition to learn. He should be trained to walk on a leash, stay, come and sit. Off lead, the dog must be trained to the extent of stopping an undesirable behavior when given a firm "no." Coming when off lead is an ideal trait, but heeling and sitting off lead are not always necessary. A dog that wants to receive commands, fetch sticks or have his belly rubbed all the time is not likely to become a good livestock guardian.

Children should not be allowed to play with a young dog that is intended for livestock protection. The puppy will easily bond to the children and end up a family pet. This should be permitted only if you want a family or general property guardian. On the other hand, the dog should be familiar and friendly with all family members.

Most livestock protection dogs, like these Akbash Dogs, prefer high vantage points to survey their territory. The large bales also provide a fun place to play. Photo by Diane Spisak.

As mentioned earlier, you would probably be disappointed if you were to expect a livestock protection dog to also be a family dog. Nor should you expect this dog to instantly work in strange surroundings or with livestock that have not been exposed to a protection dog before. Protection dogs will be decidedly unfriendly toward any other canine that enters the field containing "his" livestock. Therefore, do not expect a protection dog to make an exception for the farm herding dogs or family pets, unless they have grown up together or special socialization sessions have been arranged. Similarly, it would be unreasonable to punish a dog that tried to defend his flock from a person that rough-handled the animals, say, at shearing time, or with a cattle prod.

THE EFFECTIVENESS OF LIVESTOCK PROTECTION DOGS

In the 1970s the United States Department of Agriculture (USDA) funded research to determine the efficacy of livestock protection dogs. Several breeds were tested at the U.S. Sheep Experiment Station in Dubois, Idaho, under the supervision of Drs. Jeff Green and Roger Woodruff. Their dogs were working under minimal direction, covering huge areas, often trying to protect sheep so scattered that it was impossible to keep track of

A Texas rancher noticed one morning that his animals were unusually quiet. In fact, he couldn't find them. Walking down to the goat pens, where the Angoras would normally be crowding about for grain, there was not a creature to be found. Farther down a goat path, around a patch of woods and toward the farm pond, he found pools of blood, swatches of fur and one, two,. . .eventually seven dead coyotes. His goats were huddled in a corner of the pasture. A lone protection dog was still walking tight circles around them. Not one goat had been injured, but two of his three livestock protection dogs were dead. A wildlife officer estimated, based on prior sightings, footprints and the number of coyotes found dead of bite wounds over the next few days, that the three dogs had held off an attack of twenty or more coyotes.

them. Considering the great handicaps, many, but not all of the dogs, performed well. Livestock protection dogs are now part of the management system of the Station. In 1988, Drs. Green and Woodruff published results of a survey of almost 400 livestock protection dog users, assessing 763 dogs. They concluded that all of the major breeds and their hybrids worked equally well, with no significant difference in the effectiveness of males and females, intact or neutered. Dogs were rated as seventy-one percent very effective, twenty-one percent somewhat effective and eight percent not effective as deterrents to predators. Livestock protection dogs were considered to be an economic asset by eighty-two percent of the producers who responded. Later studies suggested that neutered dogs did perform somewhat better since they were not distracted by hormonal cycles. Currently, over fifty percent of the sheep ranchers in the western United States use livestock protection dogs as part of their management programs.

The USDA investigators also concluded that although the various breeds surveyed were comparable in terms of overall effectiveness, there were breed differences in their likeliness to bite or injure livestock and/or people and to stay with livestock. Finally, success seemed to improve when pups were raised with livestock from an age of two months or younger.

Another group that has done pioneering work with livestock protection dogs is based at Hampshire College in Massachusetts. Dr. Ray and Lorna Coppinger and their associates imported traditional livestock protection breeds for leasing to farms and ranches throughout the United States and Canada. They kept extensive records to determine the causes for success and failure of the dogs in various situations. One of their findings suggests that eighty percent or more of the dogs that fail in their first placement can be successful in a second setting. The group has been involved in reintroducing livestock guardians to European countries that have lost this old tradition. The Coppingers also introduced livestock protection dogs to countries such as Argentina and Namibia where they had never been used before. Publications resulting from both the USDA and Hampshire College studies are listed in the Bibliography.

With your appetite to learn more about the breeds hopefully whetted, we'll proceed into more detail in the succeeding chapters. Keep an open mind as to individual dogs' variations and the unique needs of each farm management system. If you can teach yourself to appreciate each situation from the dog's point of view, you'll be able to successfully train most puppies belonging to the established livestock protection breeds.

The Breeds

Livestock protection breeds are among the most ancient breeds of dogs. In fact, the role of flock guardian may have been one of the first uses humans found for the domesticated dog. Livestock protection dogs probably originated in the Middle East or Asia. This is not surprising, considering that livestock were first domesticated there. Histories of these dogs are replete with references to the earliest civilizations in Sumeria, Assyria, Mesopotamia and Kurdistan, regions that are now found in Turkey, Iran and Iraq. Drawings from before and around the time of Christ depict shepherds, their flocks, and dogs that resemble the modern guardian breeds. A passage in the Book of Job (30:1) refers to dogs as guardians of the flocks.

Slovakian Cuvac at work. Photo by Robin Rigg.

11

Nomadic tribes routinely used dogs to protect the flocks of sheep and goats they depended on for food and clothing.

Since the history of livestock protection breeds of dogs is likely to parallel that of sheep, one could approach the topic by studying the historical movements of sheep. M. L. Ryder did just that, in his 1983 book Sheep and Man. While his references to protection dogs are not extensive, they indicate that mastiff-like dogs were used in ancient Assyria and Babylonia to protect sheep from wolves, as well as to guard the house. Persians of biblical times actually had laws protecting their sheep guardian dogs and family watchdogs from abuse. Ancient Egyptians developed separate breeds of dogs for herding and guarding flocks.

Many of the breeds we shall describe are white, probably the result of selective breeding. One can speculate that white dogs blend in with sheep better and are more easily distinguished from predators by both sheep and shepherds. Then again, the selection may have been based on nothing more than human fancy. White dogs have always had a special place in myths, folklore and traditions. For instance, Babylonian diviners believed that if a white dog entered a temple it would endure forever, whereas a red dog meant the gods would depart.

Catherine de la Cruz, a breeder of Great Pyrenees, researched another theory to explain color variations. She believes that dogs were selected to have the color of the animals they protected, and that availability of water

A small pack of livestock protection dogs was given the formidable task of guarding sheep in hilly, dense forest conditions. Cougars, bears, wolves and coyotes were abundant. The wolves learned that if they could taunt a single dog into the woods, they could outnumber and kill the dog. The dogs, meanwhile, with a little help from the shepherds, learned to work in teams. Some patrolled the perimeter, while other dogs remained with the flock as fore-guards or hind-guards. Some dogs lay about at base camp until they heard a bark. A few dogs went looking, listening and sniffing for predators. After initial losses, the optimal combinations of shepherds, herding dogs, protection dogs and strategies were established. Sheep predation declined to near zero.

and clothing dyes determined the desired color of wool. Tibetan Mastiffs, for example, range from black to reddish to brown in color. So do the yaks and goats they have traditionally protected. Eastern Turkey and Syria are very dry. Sheep from this region are colored, their wool predominantly found in shades of brown and black. The protection dogs from these areas are generally fawn or gray in color with black masks. Where water was more plentiful and readily available in western Turkey and Europe, it could be used for the dying of cloth. Thus, white wool was preferred, as it could be dyed to any color. Western Turkey is the home of the Akbash Dog and most of the European livestock protection breeds are white.

There is much speculation on the origin of the various breeds. If they did indeed follow the pattern of domestication of livestock, it is possible that they spread out into different regions of the world accompanying the nomadic stockmen who kept them. They may also have accompanied horsemen during war and fought in wars, or came along with livestock intended to feed the armies. Trade routes such as the "Silk Road" connecting Europe and Asia allowed for other paths of migration and distribution. Geographical and political boundaries, as well as selection for certain traits such as the colors discussed above, would easily account for the variety of breeds we see today. Even so, there are still many disputes as to what constitutes the modern breeds. We have "lumpers" and "splitters"—the former believe that all similar dogs from a region should be regarded as a single breed, whereas the latter feel that regional variations should be respected and considered as separate breeds. The Coppingers support the former view in their book Dogs. We present a few of these discussions with our breed descriptions. Regardless of definitions, the fact remains that livestock protection dogs evolved, under human direction, to fill a need. The "experiment" has been most successful and enduring.

SPECIFIC BREEDS

We would like to stress, before beginning the description of specific breeds, that similarities between the breeds are far greater than any differences. Often there are more differences between pups in any one litter than between the breeds themselves. On the other hand, there are some traits possessed by certain breeds and not by others. We will try to point out these different features, but we will not rate the breeds as better or worse. Each situation and owner will have specific requirements and wishes, and these should be kept in mind when making a selection. In addition to breed traits, factors such as proximity, availability, breeder reputation and cost must be considered. Also, this is meant to be a brief overview of each breed. For more complete information, check out the Bibliography and search the internet for livestock dog associations, breed clubs and breeders. This information is constantly changing and being updated.

The Turkish Breeds

Amongst the oldest breeds are those that come from Turkey. We may never know the origins of these dogs because we are not aware of any written records dating back that far. Pictorial (bas-relief) evidence discovered in Turkey and the Middle East suggests a heavy-boned, ancient mastiff-type dog may have contributed to the breeds used by shepherds today.

There is no national registry for dogs in Turkey. As a result, when the first dogs were imported into North America in the early 1970s, there was confusion about how to classify and name Turkish shepherd dogs. In Turkey, the term coban kopegi, which means "shepherd's dog," is used to denote all the dogs used to protect sheep, and distinguishes them from other types of dogs, such as sighthounds, hunting dogs or urban mongrels. Turks will also use the terms Akbash, Akkush, Kangal and Karabash to denote regional breeds and specific types of livestock guardians. The first Turkish dogs imported into the United States were brought from the Anatolian plateau of Turkey and were named Anatolian Shepherd Dogs. Later importers chose to distinguish between dogs from various regions by coloration and other physical characteristics as well as locally established names. The all-white dogs, known as Akbash Dogs, are primarily from western Turkey, while fawn dogs with black masks, known as Kangal Dogs, come from the area of the Sivas province further east.

Communication between villages in the Turkish countryside has been, until recently, highly limited. Even today we find that villagers may know very little about the dogs of an adjoining town. However, there have always been people who travel to other villages and districts to visit relatives or conduct trade, and who bring the occasional pup home. Most dogs are bred from local stock, with little interaction between villages. Dogs from distant regions can be strikingly different. For instance, Akbash Dogs in western Turkey are white, and tend to be somewhat lighter in structure with more refined heads than the heavier, darker, masked Kangal Dogs of the east. Further east are pockets of Kurdish dogs, with entirely black heads and stockier bodies than the dogs in the west. And still farther east, near the border with Georgia, one finds dogs of the Caucasion Ovcharka type, which may be a distinct breed as well, referred to as Kars Dogs by some. Despite the confusion and difficulty faced by the original importers of Turkish livestock dogs in describing breeds and choosing names, the progeny of these imported dogs are performing very well outside of their native Turkey.

The Akbash Dog

The Akbash Dog is an all-white dog from western Turkey. The word akbash means "white head" in Turkish, distinguishing these dogs from the karabash or "black-headed" dogs. They are often referred to as Akkush dogs by the Turks, a term which means "white bird." This is an apt description of this sleek, fleet-footed dog. At least two distinct types of dogs may be the ancestors of the modern livestock protection dogs of Turkey: a mastiff-type dog used for guard work and possibly for war, and coursing hounds. The latter were likely the ancestors of the Tazi, or Turkish Greyhound, which can still be found in Turkey today. Of the livestock protection breeds, the Akbash Dog shows the greatest influence of the sighthound ancestry.

In Turkey, Akbash Dogs have not been kept as housepets, although we did observe "retired" dogs living in villages. They are strictly working dogs, considered essential to the security of the flocks. In their native land they protect against marauding wolves, wild dogs, jackals and bears. For centuries survival of the fittest has been the rule, and even during our visits we noted that nutritional and veterinary care was minimal by North American standards. In Turkey Akbash Dogs often wear spiked iron collars for protection in combat. Ears may be cropped to prevent torn ears when fighting. Sometimes even tails are docked.

The Akbash Dog is one of the most beautiful of the livestock guardians. He combines elegance with power. The breed is noted for its speed and agility, as well as stamina when patrolling huge tracts of land. Like the sighthounds many of them resemble, Akbash Dogs have extraordinarily keen eyesight. Mature males stand 29-32 inches (74-81 cm) at the shoulder and weigh about 120 pounds (55 kg). Females are smaller and typically have finer features. They stand 27-30 inches (68-76 cm) and tip the scales at about 90 pounds (41 kg). The Akbash Dog's double coat comes in either long or medium length versions. The plumed tail is carried low when the dog is at rest, but curls over the back when the dog moves or is alert.

Three Akbash Dog bitches showing variety of body types and coats from smooth coat, sighthound type at top, long smooth coat on intermediate type in middle, heavy long coat on mastiff type at bottom. Photos by Orysia Dawydiak and Diane Spisak (middle).

Proud Turkish owner shows off his male Akbash Dog wearing a spiked iron collar. Photo by Orysia Dawydiak.

Akbash Dogs at work guarding sheep on British Columbia cut blocks, regions where clear cutting is followed by reforestation. If you examine this photo carefully, you'll note that the "bumps" on the hill are sheep. They graze on the weeds and grasses that would otherwise choke fledgling trees. If you look even more closely, you may be able to spot a herding dog. Caring for sheep in dense forest conditions requires a team approach that includes herding dogs, shepherds, and, of course, livestock protection dogs. Photo by Jean Tinney.

18   LIVESTOCK PROTECTION DOGS

The Akbash Dog is a rare breed and is currently recognized by the United Kennel Club of the United States. Owners and breeders of working dogs do not seek wider recognition since they wish to see the working abilities of the breed maintained. Akbash Dogs have proved popular since their introduction to North America in the late 1970s and there are many now serving as effective guardians. They have proven valuable as deterrents to coyotes, feral dogs, bears and cougars.

The Anatolian Shepherd Dog

The Anatolian Shepherd Dog is the most popular of the Turkish breeds in North America. The breed shares the same historical background

Well-balanced Anatolian Shepherd Dogs, fawn with black masks, illustrating the difference between male and female body types. Photos by Jennifer Floyd (male) and Henry Ballester (female).

Fine male
Anatolian
Shepherd with
pinto coloration.
Photo by Marsha
Peterson.

and traditional working qualities as the Akbash and Kangal Dogs. The clubs
that promote Anatolian Shepherd Dogs take an all-encompassing view of
coloration. They register all colors and allow those who so wish to special-
ize in individual colors. The majority of recent imports have come from the
Sivas region of Turkey so they are often indistinguishable from the Kangal
Dog. In the United States the breed is recognized by the United Kennel
Club as well as the American Kennel Club, and in Europe by the Federation
Cynologique Internationale.

Anatolians are regarded as flock guardians of the mountain
Molossian-type. Large and rugged, they possess great endurance and agility. Males stand 29-32 inches (74-81 cm) tall and weigh 110-140 pounds (50-
64 kg). Bitches are 27-31 inches (69-79 cm) tall and weigh 90-120 pounds
(41-55 kg). The outer coat is short or half-long, dense and tends to increase
in the winter. The undercoat is thick. There are great variations in length
of outer coat, although very short smooth coats or long, hanging coats are
considered faults. Anatolians are described as being bold and confident, and
not easily overstimulated. The dogs are loyal and affectionate without being
overly demonstrative with family, yet aloof and suspicious of strangers.

The Anatolian Shepherd Dog is a commendable livestock protector
and home guardian. This was one of the breeds included in the program at

These Anatolian Shepherd pups are all littermates from a white dam and a brindle sire and show some of the color variation found in this breed. Photo by Jennifer Floyd.

Hampshire College. Although they are shown in conformation competitions, the breed standard for the United Kennel Club lists as one disqualification a dog incapable of guarding livestock. This is a logical requirement for a working breed and should probably be included for all livestock protection dogs promoted as such.

The Kangal Dog

The Kangal Dog is the rarest of the Turkish breeds outside of its native country. Many Kangal Dogs and Kangal-crosses that fit the breed description are registered as Anatolian Shepherds. Kangal Dogs may also be referred to as Karabash. Elisabeth von Buchwaldt, who has traveled extensively across the Middle East and Asia studying the livestock protection breeds, reports that many countries have their own versions of Karabash (black-headed livestock guardians). She has seen and photographed Karabash-type dogs in Iran, Azerbaijan, Turkmenistan and even Kosovo. Today, the Karabash dogs of the Sivas region are called Kangal Dogs. The breed is famous in Turkey, and many consider Kangal Dogs to be a national treasure. To understand how valuable these dogs are to their owners, one needs only to read the description of W. J. Childs' travels through the region in the early 1900s. He was terrified of these "country dogs" who were "the largest and most savage of any I had met. In build they were like Newfoundlands, but larger, with black head or muzzle, yellow body and long curling tail." (Childs, 1917). Though he longed to shoot the dogs on sight, he dared not because he wrote that they were protected by Turkish law and even more so by custom. To shoot a dog was to risk his own life.

To this day it is nearly impossible to convince rural Turkish owners to part with their finest dogs, and exporting out of the country can be very difficult. The breed attracts much media attention and has even appeared on national postal stamps. There is a Kangal Dog Festival held in the town of Kangal, Sivas province, each July to honor their indigenous breed. For residents of the area, this has become the cultural event of the year.

The base coat color of Kangal Dogs ranges from cream to light tan, with varying amounts of dark guard hairs mixed in; these can, when abundant, give the dog an overall gray appearance. All have the characteristic black mask, which on some dogs can extend to cover the head. Dogs stand

Turkish shepherd with four Kangal Dogs in Doymus Village, Sivas province. Notice the cropped ears and spiked collars. Photo by Sue Kocher.

Top: A sign at the entrance to Sivas province, Turkey which reads, "You are at the agricultural administration directorate. Kangal Dog Breeding Station." Bottom: A sign in the town of Kangal welcoming visitors to the Kangal Shepherd's Dog Festival. Photos by Elisabeth von Buchwaldt.

29-33 inches (74-84 cm) tall and weigh 110-150 pounds (50-68 kg). Bitches are 27-31 inches (69-79 cm) tall and weigh 90-125 pounds (41-57 kg). The coat is short and dense, with a thick undercoat. It is slightly longer at the neck and shoulders, and its texture is soft. Rear dewclaws, even double dewclaws, are common. In Turkey, ears are often cropped, although that practice is not carried on outside the country. In the United States, the Kangal Dog is recognized by the United Kennel Club.

Two lovely Kangal Dog bitches, Ceylan and Talihli, on a peat moor in Germany. Photo by Elisabeth von Buchwaldt.

Temperament of the Kangal Dog is similar to the other Turkish breeds. One subtle difference between this dog and the Akbash Dog is that the Kangal appears slightly more tractable than the Akbash, and may be easier to train and control. Conversely, the Akbash Dog is more independent-minded. However, the differences are not huge, and individual dogs may display just the opposite features. There are very few Kangal Dogs guarding livestock in North America today, but as their numbers increase, this will likely change. Based on their excellent working reputation in Turkey, there is no reason why Kangal Dogs should not do as well here.

The Caucasian Ovcharka

The Caucasian Ovcharka—also known as the Caucasian Shepherd or Sheepdog, Caucasian Mountain Dog, Kavkazkaya Ovcharka, Kaukasische Schaferhund, Nagazi and Volkodav—was originally bred to guard the flocks of the Caucasus Mountains. The harsh conditions and geographical location of the native area resulted in a large, aggressive breed suited to the

Tibor, a young male Caucasian Ovcharka, accompanies his sheep on their Saskatchewan pastures. Photo by Orysia Dawydiak.

work required. The Caucasian Ovcharka is considered a "natural" breed, indigenous to the region for which it was named. Further selection by the Soviet Military produced a more trainable and compliant service dog. The Caucasian today is a magnificent guarding breed, sweet and gentle with family but tough and aggressive to strangers.

Due to their outstanding abilities as territorial guard dogs and high demand for guarding factories and warehouses, as well as their limited bloodlines, Caucasians were crossed with a number of breeds such as the Leonberger, Saint Bernard, German Shepherd and Great Dane. As a result, breed experts estimate that up to eighty percent of the current population in the former Soviet Republics are mixed-breed dogs. Today, pure bloodlines are expensive and difficult to get past customs, although there are now at least sixteen distinct bloodlines in North America.

Physically, it is the head of the Caucasian Ovcharka which sets this breed apart from other heavily furred mastiffs. The head is massive, with a broad skull and strongly developed cheekbones. High-set, cropped ears, oblique eyes and a deep, wedge-shaped muzzle completes the picture.

Tszakar, a male Caucasian, likes to sit atop high vantage points to guard more effectively. Photo by Thunder Hawk Caucasians.

Coats are double-layered and slightly off-standing and come in three acceptable coat lengths: short, medium and long, the latter with excessive fringing on the pantaloons and tail. A distinctive black mask and "spectacles" around the eyes are desirable. The outer coat, or guard hairs, are black, with the undercoat ranging in color from steel-gray to straw-colored, to red. One may also see a "clear fawn" without black guard hairs and with or without the mask; brindle; ticking; and varying amounts of white patching from white socks or chest up to extreme white piebalds. Solid black, black-and-tan, or Saint Bernard red-and-white are not acceptable colors.

Caucasian Ovcharkas should be a minimum of 26 inches (66 cm) at the shoulder, preferably larger. The typical male is 30 inches (76 cm) tall and weighs 120 pounds (55 kg) or more. Females are about 28 inches (71 cm) and weigh 90 to 120 pounds (41-55 kg), and are distinctly lighter in build. The neck is powerful and short, the chest is broad and deep, and the abdomen is moderately tucked. The tail is high-set, hanging downward, and carried as a sickle-shaped hook or ring when raised in excitement or gaiting. The characteristic gait is a short prancing trot.

Relative to other flock guardian breeds, Caucasian Ovcharkas are more aggressive and more trainable as a result of their selection for military work. They are not recommended as companion dogs except in cases where there is a true need for personal and property protection. There are a few that successfully guard livestock; however, they must be chosen carefully, and they prefer to work more closely with people than some of the other breeds. Experienced, ethical breeders can differentiate between pups with less aggression, who are perhaps less socially inclined and may be better suited to work with livestock. Breeders are also working on decreasing the high incidence of hip dysplasia which afflicts the breed. The Caucasian is considered to be a long-lived breed, reaching twelve years and older. It is recognized by the United Kennel Club in the United States and the Federation Cynologique Internationale in Europe.

The Great Pyrenees

The Great Pyrenees, also known as the Pyrenean Mountain Dog, originated in the Pyrenees Mountains along the border between France and Spain. This is probably the best known and most popular of the livestock protection breeds in North America. For hundreds of years, these huge, heavy-coated dogs have been known to guard sheep in the mountains, as well as the chateaux of the French nobility. In the fifteenth century, they assisted guards on sentry duty. In 1675 the Great Pyrenees was adopted as the Royal Dog of France by the Dauphin, Louis XIV, and became sought after by nobility. Great Pyrenees also acted as pack animals in the mountains and message carriers. The dogs were often found lying across the doorways of their peasant masters and became known as "mat dogs." They also had been used to pull milk carts until relatively recent times.

During the 1920s the breed suffered a decline in numbers in its native France. A few dedicated breeders joined to form the "Reunion des Amateurs de Chiens Pyreneens," which still exists. They began the difficult job of reconstituting the breed and building up the numbers again. Travelling to remote mountain villages, they collected a few dogs that they felt truly represented the best of the breed. The breed standard they published in 1927 formed the basis for all the current standards.

Taken in the 1950s, this photo shows a Great Pyrenees accompanying two shepherds and the flock belonging to Phil and Shirley Kern down a road in Washington state. Photo provided by John and Kerry Kern-Woods.
(bottom) A handsome male Great Pyrenees, Gimlet, keeps an eye out for trouble outside his owner's yard. Photo by Karen Justin.

The first dogs to be imported into the United States came in 1824. General Lafayette brought two males to his friend, J. S. Skinner, author of The Dog and the Sportsman. However, there was not much heard about the breed until the next century, when Mary and Francis Crane established the first U.S. kennel in the early 1930s. The Cranes imported over sixty dogs from Europe, and certainly helped maintain bloodlines which would have been decimated by the Second World War. In 1933

Great Pyrenees, Sadie, with llama, Tessie, checking each other out. Photo by Janice Reed.

the Great Pyrenees was recognized by the American Kennel Club. The Great Pyrenees Club of America was formed in the 1930s, is the oldest in North America, and is well organized, having numerous affiliated regional associations, a livestock protection dog program, and a network of rescue organizations to care for abandoned or lost dogs.

The Great Pyrenees is a most impressive and beautiful breed. Primarily white in color, the coat may have markings of badger, gray or varying shades of tan. The weather-resistant double coat consists of a long, flat, thick, outer coat of coarse hair, straight or slightly undulating, lying over a dense, fine, woolly undercoat. The head is not heavy in proportion to the size of the dog, it is wedge-shaped with a slightly rounded crown. There is no apparent stop. The tail is well plumed, is carried low in repose and may or may not be carried over the back when gaiting. Double dewclaws are a feature of the rear legs. Males stand 27 to 32 inches (69-81 cm) tall and weigh 100 pounds (45 kg) or more. Bitches are 25-29 inches (63-74 cm) tall and weigh 85 pounds (39 kg) or more.

Great Pyrenees have been used to guard stock in North America since the late 1940s. A 1951 newspaper article and photo in the Spokesman-Review of Washington state describes Pyrenees livestock guardians at work. They have been used successfully since then to protect a variety of livestock from a variety of predators. The Great Pyrenees Club of America differentiates between "Ranch or Farm Dogs" and "Livestock Guardian Dogs" within their breed. The former is part pet, part guardian; the latter is expected to work more independently and sometimes in semi-isolation. They suggest that it is best to select a pup from parents that have proven themselves in the conditions in which the pup is expected to work. There are lines and individuals that may have a softer temperament than others, and although most will guard against wild predators, some are less aggressive towards domestic dogs. The Great Pyrenees tends to accept human strangers more readily than most of the other breeds. Overall, this is a fine working breed, with an estimated three to five percent of the approximately 80,000 Great Pyrenees in the United States actively guarding livestock.

The Komondor

The Komondor is one of the more distinctive livestock guardian breeds. He has been guarding flocks on the steppes of Hungary for hundreds of

Hart, a male Komondor in a six-year-old show coat. This type of coat would not be seen on a working dog. Photo by Lyn Bingham.

Venusz has had her coat shorn, as are the coats of many working Komondorok. Photo by Lyn Bingham.

years. It is believed that the Komondor was the dog of the Kuns (also known as the Cumans or Komans), a Turkic-speaking people originally from northeastern Asia in the Mongolian plains. The nomadic Kuns were invaded by the Mongols, who also expanded their raids into eastern and central Europe in the thirteenth century. The Kuns eventually relocated to the plains of Hungary (putza), which resembled their homeland. They remained culturally distinct from the Magyar people who co-inhabited Hungary, which may explain why this country continues to support two distinct breeds of livestock protection dogs, the Komondor and the Kuvasz.

Upon maturity, there is no mistaking this breed for any of the other livestock guardians. His full white coat hangs in long tassels, or cords, all over his body. These dogs have had to withstand extreme heat and cold, living outside in a harsh climate year-round. In fact, the heavy coat is best suited to the drier conditions of the flat, open plains of their ancestral home. As well as providing insulation from the elements, it also protects them from injury during battles with wolves and other predators. The

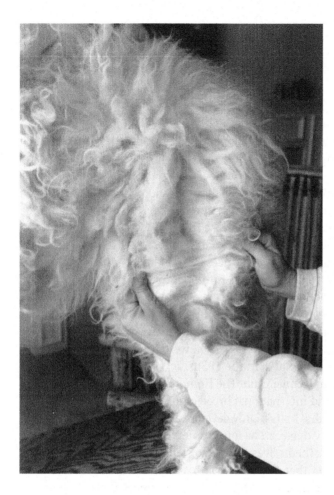

Cording is a controlled form of matting. Mats begin between nine to twelve months of age. Hand splitting to separate clumps into cords is done by gripping the coat and pulling it apart. Photo by Lyn Bingham.

continually growing guard hairs that trap underlying insulation hairs produce the ever-lengthening cords.

Males in North America average 27-28 inches (69-71 cm) at the shoulder, with females being at least 25 $1/2$ inches (64 cm) tall. The average male Komondor will mature to between 85 and 100 pounds (39-45 kg), although the thick coat makes him appear much larger. Caring properly for a corded coat can take a long time, and if the coat is not corded regularly it may mat in sheets. Some working dog owners prefer to keep their dogs clipped, especially during summer months. It is also recommended that hair between the food pads be kept clipped to prevent accumulation of burrs or irritation and infection. Ear canals tend to fill with dirt and hair and should be cleaned often. Other health problems are those typical for the large breeds, but buyers should ask about hip certification, bloat, entropion and cataract incidence in the bloodlines. Life expectancy is about twelve years.

Komondorok (the plural of Komondor) are among the more aggressive of the livestock guardian breeds, so it is especially important to socialize them well as youngsters. If left alone to guard stock, they will be highly suspicious of any new people. As puppies, they can be quite playful and must be monitored carefully with livestock. Once they are bonded to their charges, Komondorok are extremely devoted and protective. This even extends to their sex life—it is not uncommon for them to become so attached to their "mates" that they refuse to breed with less familiar dogs.

Another interesting trait is in the Komondor's guarding style, which may have developed as a result of ancestral conditions on the plains. As opposed to dogs that actively patrol, Komondorok are typically sedentary guardians. They select strategic points of land where they can lie while viewing a large area. A disturbance results in quick reaction as the dog jumps up to investigate and repel any threats to his charges.

Like the Great Pyrenees, Komondorok were first imported into North America in significant numbers in the 1930s. In 1937 the breed was recognized by the American Kennel Club. The Komondor is now recognized by all the major national and international breed clubs, and is shown widely. Still not a common breed due to its highly developed protective instinct, breeders feel that good working dogs can be found amongst litters whose parents are not guarding livestock themselves. They also claim that the Komondor is less likely to wander than other breeds of livestock guardians. However, due to their strong protective nature, fencing is still recommended.

The Kuvasz

Kuvaszok (the plural of Kuvasz) are also from Hungary and have luxuriant, medium-long, all-white coats. They resemble the Akbash Dog in many ways, and may indeed be descended from the dogs of old Kurdistan, the area now delineated by Turkey, Syria and Iraq. The word Kuvasz may be derived from a Turkish word, kavas, meaning safekeeper or guard. Another theory suggests that the word may arise from Chuvash, the ancient agrarians of the steppes where Hungary is today. It is clear that the breed has existed for hundreds of years, protecting livestock against wolves, bears and thieves; hunting big game; helping during war; and most recently, as a guardian of estates, homes and property.

Two Kuvasz bitches, best friends Huseg and Bodri, pause after a romp. Photo by Afiena Kamminga.

In the late 1400s the popularity of the Kuvasz peaked under the reign of Hungarian King Matthias I. The king was said to have trusted his dogs more than his own servants. He always kept a dog in his company, had them guarding people, and livestock, and used them to hunt boar, bears and wolves. The Kuvasz came to be regarded as the "armed guard of royalty."

During World War II, the breed was nearly decimated by advancing armies that killed thousands of dogs. More dogs starved to death during the food shortages which followed. By the early 1950s only twelve dogs could be located in Hungary to rebuild the population. Fortunately, there were dogs outside of Europe, the breed having appeared in North America in the 1920s.

Kuvasz males stand about 29 inches (74 cm) tall and weigh 90-115 pounds (41-52 kg). Bitches are about 27 inches (69 cm) tall and weigh 65-90 pounds (30-41 kg). They are not a massive dog and should appear lean and lithe. The thick double coat typically is wavy with crests and swirls. Although the breed standard calls for it, a mane is not always present, unlike some of the other breeds. Skin pigment is dark and coat is always white with no markings. The head is finely chiselled, with dark, almond-shaped eyes and dark nose, and a stop only slightly marked. Lips and eyelids are tight; the hair covering the skull and ears is short. The tail is well plumed and carried low unless the dog is excited, when it will curl up to the level of the loin. This is a hardy, natural breed that does well in cold and tolerates heat.

Kuvaszok are sensitive to praise and blame. They are gentle towards their family and very protective of small children and animals they have been raised with. They tend to be a one-family dog and highly suspicious of strangers. Therefore, they must be well socialized if they are expected to tolerate much human traffic wherever they live.

The Kuvasz is recognized by the American and Canadian Kennel Clubs, and there are several Kuvasz clubs in North America. Most of these clubs promote the breed for show, work and companionship. They feel that the breed's protective instinct has never been lost. Although the dogs were developed as livestock guardians, there are very few working in this capacity in North America today. Compared with a breed like the Great Pyrenees, the Kuvasz may be more active, more aggressive and quicker to attack. Those Kuvaszok that are guarding stock are reported to be doing an excellent job.

The Maremma Sheepdog

From the Abruzzi region of the Appenine Mountains of central Italy and the Maremma Plains comes another large, rough-coated breed, the Maremmano-Abruzzese. Outside of Italy, the breed is known as the Maremma Sheepdog. Also thought to be descended from the great white sheep guardians of the Middle East, originally two types were found in Italy. The longer-bodied, longer-haired mountain dog, the Abruzzese, and the Maremmano of the plains were combined to create a single breed with a hyphenated name in the 1950s.

Maremma Sheepdogs stand 24 to 29 inches (61-74 cm) tall and weigh 65 to 100 pounds (30-45 kg). They are white but can have some shading of ivory, lemon or pale orange. The coat is thick and long with a slight wave. Ears are v-shaped and rather small. Eyes should be dark, and lips, nose and eyerims should be black. The tail is set low, reaching below the hocks. It is carried down when the dog is relaxed, but becomes level with the back when he is alert, the tip gently curved.

Maremma Sheepdogs have proved to be excellent working dogs under many conditions. They do best in farm situations rather than alone

Catone, a working Maremma. Photo by Agostino Molinelli.

on the range, although they can be left with unattended flocks. Traditionally, they worked under the supervision of shepherds by day and remained with flocks in smaller enclosures by night. In Italy flocks of up to 300 animals are milked twice a day and are often moved from the lower plains to the mountains during the summer months. Although wolves and some brown bears continue to prey on sheep, the primary threat comes from feral dogs. Maremma Sheepdogs have proven effective against all of these predators and are still used widely in Italy to protect sheep, goats and other livestock.

Historically, Maremmas also served a role as estate guardians, especially in Tuscany. The Maremma Sheepdog Club does not recommend this breed for a companion dog, although it can fulfill that purpose in the right

In the Gran Sasso mountains of central Italy, the Maremma is still an important member of the flock. Photo by Ray Coppinger.

environment, with knowledgeable owners. The club estimates that ninety percent of North American Maremmas live in working situations today.

The Polish Tatra Sheepdog

In its homeland of Poland, the breed is also known as Owczarek Podhalanski. This can be translated into shepherd dog of the Podhale, a region of Poland which includes Tatras range in the Carpathian Mountains. Another huge white dog with a heavy double coat, Tatras at 26 to 28 inches (66-71 cm) for males and 24 to 26 inches (61-66 cm) for females, stand a little shorter than some of the other breeds. However, they weigh 80-130 pounds (36-59 kg) and can still be found guarding sheep in their native country.

As with a number of other European breeds, the Polish Tatra was nearly wiped out during the Second World War. Many dogs were taken out of the country to be lost forever. The breed was slowly built back up after the war, but their use to guard livestock declined. In recent years, especially with the reintroduction of wolves into southern Poland, the breed has enjoyed a resurgence and numbers are growing again. At the present, there are about 300 dogs in Poland, with about 150 in North America, and of those approximately 20 are guarding livestock. The Tatra has also been used in Poland for police, military and guide dog work, as well as for personal protection, to guard factories and to haul carts.

Polish Tatra Sheepdogs are all white with black pigmented nose, lips and dark foot pads. The eyes are dark brown, the eyerims are dark. The top coat is hard to the touch and straight or slightly wavy. The undercoat is profuse and dense. The tail hangs below the topline, but when the dog is excited it is carried above the back, though not curved.

Perhaps the most interesting traits of the Polish Tatra are found in the character of the breed. Tatras are described as being extremely smart and intuitive, often out-thinking their owners. They use vocalizations and facial expressions to communicate, especially their pleasure. They tend to be flock-oriented rather than territorial and generally do not give chase to predators. Tatras work best under the direction of shepherds and may not be as suited to open-range conditions as other more independent breeds. They are generally people-friendly and not as dog-aggressive as some of the

An excellent example of an adult Polish Tatra sheepdog, Kosor z Wyskowek. Photo by Carol A. Wood.

other breeds. They also display a form of herding behavior that is somewhat more active than the alarm posturing which might draw sheep to a dog barking at a predator. Tatras have been known, under the direction of a shepherd or on their own, to round up sheep by running in tightening circles around the flock, barking and shoving them together. They can also influence the movement of the flock in the direction indicated by the shepherd by blending with the flock. They do not herd in the same sense as a Border Collie that stalks, gives eye and bites. The Tatra style of herding is apparently also common to the Slovakian Cuvac, a closely related breed.

The Polish Tatra Sheepdog remains one of the more rare livestock protection breeds, but shows great promise, particularly with highly managed flocks and situations where livestock are kept in closer quarters or are moved frequently.

The Slovakian Cuvac

Also known as the Tatra Cuvac (pronounced Choo-vach), Slovensky Cuvac or Liptok, named after a mountain range, this breed resembles and is related to the Kuvasz and Polish Tatra Sheepdog. In the country we know as Slovakia, the Cuvac was historically used as a watch dog, a guide for shepherds, a cattle guardian and also to drive poultry and other stock to pasture. More recently, they have been used to guard and drive milking sheep and to keep sheep in designated grazing areas, often near more populated centers. Older shepherds recall seeing Cuvac grab and hold individual sheep on command, and even track lost sheep. Unfortunately, the previous generation of shepherds who trained dogs for these tasks are long gone and it appears that those specific training methods are now lost.

A visitor who interviewed some of the modern shepherds milking sheep tells us that the word "cuvac" is a specific shepherd's command that requires the dog to go ahead of a herd and stop it from moving. The dogs are also clever enough to know when predators should only be warned off with barking or chased away. Given the unusual herding abilities, and the breed's higher activity level, it is not hard to believe that the Cuvac may indeed have Spitz blood, and perhaps that of other breeds, crossed with the native white mountain dogs. In appearance they are similar to the Kuvasz. Males stand 24 to 28 inches (61-71 cm) tall and bitches 23 to 26 inches (58-66 cm). The outer coat is often wavy and two to six inches long. The skin is pink except for black pigmentation around the eyes and the muzzle, and on the pads.

Blanca (female) and Axo (male), a Slovakian Cuvac pair, protect their flock in Slovakia near the Ukrainian border. Photo by Robin Rigg.

Today the breed is being reintroduced into some of the more remote regions of the Carpathian Mountains since large predators are also returning. Although they have primarily been used for estate guardians, companions, and even search and rescue and border patrol for the past several decades, it appears the Cuvac can still provide protection for herds of small stock in the high mountain pastures. The main stumbling block may be in training modern shepherds to use and trust the dogs. People involved in the conservation of large, carnivorous mammals are hopeful, however.

We currently know of very few Cuvac guarding livestock in North America, due largely to the rarity of this most interesting breed.

The Tibetan Mastiff

The Tibetan Mastiff, known as Do Khyi in Tibet, may very well be a direct descendant of one of the oldest breeds of livestock protection dogs. For over 2,000 years, this breed has been used in the high valleys and mountains of Himalayan Asia in Tibet, Nepal, Bhutan and northern India to guard flocks of sheep, goats, cattle and yaks from snow leopards, bears, tigers and wolves. They have also been kept to protect monasteries, farms,

Three Tibetan Mastiffs integrated with their flock at Fairyhill Farm, New Brunswick. Photo by Peter Vido.

military camps and other domestic compounds. Pairs of Tibetan Mastiffs guarded the four gates of the summer palace of the Dalai Lama in Lhasa.

This breed was supposedly much larger than it is today. Early explorers described the Tibetan Mastiff as being the size of a donkey, with a bark like the roar of a lion. Long cherished and respected for strength and devotion, the breed suffered from a massacre instigated by the Chinese Communist invasion in the 1950s. Today the remaining Tibetan Mastiffs are 24 to 30 inches (61-76 cm) tall and heavy-boned, weighing 90 to 170 pounds (41-77 kg). Their coat is dense, fairly long and straight, with a woolly undercoat which sheds out once a year. It can be variably colored, black being the most common, although cream, brindle or fawn dogs with black masks are not favored by the people of the Himalayas. The bushy tail usually curls over the back. A thick ruff, heavy shoulders and head, pendant ears and slightly pendulous lips are typical traits of this proud, impressive breed.

The Tibetan Mastiff is considered a primitive breed, one of the unique features being that bitches only cycle once a year, usually in the fall. They generally have low activity levels but can spring into action when called upon. They differ from the other livestock protection breeds also in one aspect of health—a proportion of the population carries a gene for a disorder called CIDN (Canine Inherited Demyelinative Neuropathy). There is no test currently available to identify carriers of this debilitating recessive disease, so test breeding remains the only way to determine that breeding stock is free. Other health problems are those typical of the other breeds. Tibetan Mastiffs appear to have a normal lifespan of ten to twelve years.

Loyal and protective, Tibetan Mastiffs can be wonderful companions to people who understand their independent nature. They have had mixed success as livestock guardians in North America. Many are too people-oriented to be content to remain with livestock. They seem to work best when people are nearby, and on smaller holdings. There is some question about the possibility that what we have in North America is a mixture of Himalayan breeds which includes the true Do Khyi and the smaller Bhotia, also known as the Himalayan Sheepdog in India. This could account for the wide range in size and working temperament. The Bhotia is known for his agility among the steep mountain slopes, and his fierceness against man and beast disturbing his charges. Do Khyi, a larger, slower dog, may be somewhat more social towards humans, although he can be equally ferocious towards four-legged predators.

Black and tan Tibetan Mastiff males on a British Columbia farm. Photo by Gabriele Gruenwald.

Today there are estimated to be up to 2,000 registered Tibetan Mastiffs in North America. Not many are working with livestock, however; those that are have proven to be effective. They tend to be territorial rather than bonding to the stock.

Other Breeds

We have not described all the breeds used to guard livestock. Breed books such as The Atlas of Dog Breeds of the World, Desmond Morris's Dogs, A Celebration of Rare Breeds and Simon and Schuster's Guide to Dogs, among many others, can provide breed descriptions of even more rare livestock guardian dog breeds. We include here brief descriptions of a few more European breeds which are currently being imported into North America.

The **Sarplaninac** of Yugoslavia has a medium length coat which is variably colored. Also called the Yugoslavian Shar Planinetz or Illyrian Sheepdog, this breed tends to be somewhat smaller than the other protection breeds at 22 to 24 inches (56-61 cm) in height. It has proven reliable within the Hampshire College dog leasing program. There are few of them in North America, so we cannot make specific comments about this breed, but in their native land, now called Macedonia, they have been used to work cattle and guard livestock for a very long time. With the fragmentation of

Sarplaninac with sheep in Oregon, Hampshire College Dog Project. Photo by Jay Lorenz.

Castro Laboreiro watches over his goat herd. Photo by Carla Cruz.

Yugoslavia into several countries, it is uncertain how the breed will be represented in the future. Currently there is no breed club in North America.

Another breed, also used by the Hampshire College dog leasing program and imported from the northern mountainous region of Portugal, is
the **Castro Laboreiro**. This breed has not been tested adequately in North
America to establish its effectiveness as a livestock protector, although a few
have worked quite well. They are short-coated dogs, colored black, or black
mixed with brown or mahogany, smaller than the other protection breeds at
20 to 24 inches (51-61 cm) tall, and resembling the Labrador Retriever. There
is in fact some speculation that the Labrador Retriever has Castro Laboreiro
in its ancestry. Being "Lab-like," they are less likely to be feared by strangers
who do not recognize their function. In their native country they have been
used primarily to guard stock, but some have also been trained to fetch stray
animals, to hunt in packs and as police and military dogs.

Also from Portugal, but from the Estrela Mountains in the central
region, comes the **Estrela Mountain Dog**. Physically, this breed resembles
the Sarplaninac, although it is a little larger at 24-28 inches (61-71 cm) with
males weighing up to 110 pounds (50 kg). The thick, rough coat is medium
to long, the colors ranging between wolf gray, fawn and yellow, both solid
and with white patches and usually with black shadings and mask. Although

The long-haired variety of Estrela Mountain Dog. Photo by Carla Cruz.

the breed went into decline during the industrial era, there has been renewed interest and a number of breed clubs now exist. In the past, the Estrela has been used to guard flocks of sheep and goats, as property guardians and as cart dogs to haul milk and cheese. They have also been trained to hunt, and have been used by the Portuguese armed forces. Currently, some are still used to guard livestock in their native country, as well as being companion dogs for owners who also want protection.

Yet another breed from Portugal is the **Rafeiro do Alentejo**, also known as the Alentejo Shepherd Dog. It is believed the origins of this breed come from a variety of other livestock guardians, including the Spanish Mastiff. The head is described as bear-like and the gait heavy and slow. The Rafeiro is the largest of the Portuguese breeds at 25-29 inches (63-74 cm) in height and weighing up to 110 pounds (50 kg). The short to medium coat is thick, smooth and dense. It may be black, gray, tan, yellow, brindle or white with colored patches. The breed was developed in the south of Portugal where it used to guard flocks. Early in the twentieth century these dogs were also part of the royal hunting packs. Since the 1950s there has been more effort put into recovering the breed.

A Rafeiro do Alentejo from Portugal. Photo by Carla Cruz.

The **Pyrenean Mastiff** from northern Spain is another rare breed of ancient livestock guardian enjoying resurgence in its native country and abroad. Originating in the Middle East, Phoenician traders brought these huge dogs to the Iberian peninsula, where they were used to guard and accompany huge flocks of sheep as they migrated between summer and winter pastures. The Pyrenean Mastiff has a rough white coat colored with patches of black, brindle, gray, orange or fawn. They stand 28-32 inches (71-81 cm) tall and weigh 120-155 pounds (55-70 kg). The head is larger than the Great Pyrenees, with more dewlap and haw showing. Calm and gentle by nature, they can be aggressive when their charges are threatened.

Mixed Breeds
The Navajo Indians of North America have been using mixed-breed dogs of non-traditional backgrounds to protect livestock for some time and with some success, as has been reported by researcher Hal Black (see the Bibliography.) There is not much to say about the Navajo program, since no particular type of dog is used, and there have been no comparisons of

Pyrenean Mastiff. Photo by Karin Graefe.

the mixed breeds' effectiveness with that of the traditional protection dog breeds. What is interesting, though, is the parallel evolution of livestock protection dogs by native Americans, during the same time that most of the recent interest in predator control in North America centers around purebred stocks of dogs from Asia and Europe.

In Europe and even in many locales in North America, the pure traditional livestock guardian breeds are being crossbred. Occasionally this is done for convenience when a rancher has two different breeds and wishes to increase the number of dogs to cover his growing flock. Some people are crossbreeding on purpose, feeling that the traits of two different breeds produce the ideal dog for their situation. Others are creating new hybrids and giving them new breed names. In Europe, there are areas where crossbreeding is the norm, such as the Rumanian hybrid dogs. Most of these dogs work as well as the purebreds, some even better. Those who promote the notion of "hybrid vigor" must keep in mind that the offspring will only be as good as what the parents have to offer. In other words, if

A Romanian shepherd with a mixed breed guard dog. Photo by Robin Rigg.

The Karakatchan, a livestock guardian native to Bulgaria, became rare during the communist regime but is now recovering thanks to Bulgarian dog enthusiasts and conservationists. Photo by Robin Rigg.

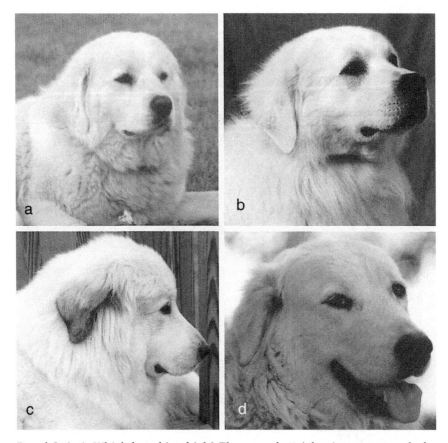

Breed Quiz 1: Which breed is which? These can be tricky. Answers at end of chapter.

they begin with purebreds who carry genetic defects, those same defects will be passed on to their pups. Breeders must still be selective when they assess their pups. Purebred or not, some will make better livestock guardians than others. One final note about cross breeding—there are a number of accidental matings between guard dogs and herding dogs. This can result in the worst possible combination of traits, an energetic, aggressive dog with the size and strength of a protection dog, programmed to chase and harass stock. Most of these dogs can never be tusted with livestock.

THE PAST AND FUTURE OF
LIVESTOCK PROTECTION BREEDS

The concept of pure breeds is actually a relatively modern phenomenon. In their recent book Dogs, the Coppingers suggest that there is a continuum of livestock guarding dogs across Europe which is maintained by transhumance, the seasonal migration of flocks and dogs across modern borders. Rather than refer to them as distinct breeds, the Coppingers suggest these dogs display regional characteristics. Physical traits and common histories support the fact that many of the livestock protection breeds are closely related. Breed distinctions are often the result of cultural, geographic and political divisions throughout Europe and Asia. DNA typing may be the only way to resolve the lively discussions and debates surrounding breed nomenclature. Recent mitochondrial DNA work has determined that dogs were first domesticated in eastern Asia around 14,000 to 15,000 years ago. This type of detective work may also elucidate the history of livestock protection dogs and support or refute a genetic distinction between the various breeds as they are currently delineated.

Sheep bonding experience. Akbash Dog puppy, Metin, lies in the manger, where interactions with sheep are inevitable. Properly supervised and appropriately rewarded, this form of behavior is the beginning of a successful bonding. Photo by Diane Spisak.

Breed Quiz 2: A little more obvious ... perhaps.

Breed Quiz 3: Some are easier to name than others.

Photo Quiz answers and photographer credits:

Quiz 1

a. Akbash Dog. Cindy Mellom.
b. Polish Tatra. Steve Rogers.
c. Great Pyrenees. Karen Justin.
d. Maremma. Agostino Molinelli.

Quiz 2

a. Kangal Dog. Gary Davis.
b. Komondor, year old. Lyn Bingham.
c. Kuvasz, six months old. Stuart Prisk.
d. Estrela Mountain Dog, short-haired variety. Carla Cruz.
e. Caucasian Ovcharka, Armenian type. Thunder Hawk Caucasians.

Quiz 3

a. Castro Laboreiro. Carla Cruz.
b. Caucasian Ovcharka. Thunder Hawk Caucasians.
c. Maremma. Agostino Molinelli.
d. Estrela Mountain Dog, long-haired variety. Carla Cruz.
e. Slovakian Cuvac. Robin Rigg.

A more pressing concern to us is the way some breed clubs empha-size the physical appearance of dogs over working temperament. Large size in particular is a trait that is often encouraged to the detriment of sound-ness and working ability. The showing of dogs in conformation competi-tions which reward breeders for producing certain types and sizes may inadvertently dilute the characteristics which are most beneficial to a working livestock guardian. In countries of origin, poor protection dogs are simply destroyed. If dogs are not selected primarily for their working abilities, within several generations there will be lines and perhaps even breeds of dogs not able to protect. Breed standards can be adhered to while maintaining the correct temperament and structure to perform the duties they were originally bred for. Breed associations that emphasize working ability rather than showing are needed if these breeds are to remain func-tional in North America and elsewhere.

CHAPTER

Selecting a Puppy

3

By now you may have narrowed your choice to one or two of the livestock protection breeds. Are there any practical reasons for choosing one breed over another? In North America, with its widely varying climates and topography, some breeds seem to do better in certain areas. Long-coated dogs do not fare as well in the hot, humid Southeast. Some people feel lighter colored dogs are better suited to the summer heat of the south. Cold isn't as much of a factor as is heat—all breeds respond to cold by growing insulating undercoats, regardless of the length of the guard hair.

From a behavioral point of view, there do seem to be a few differences between the breeds, although there can be more variability between genetic strains within a breed or even within a litter than between breeds. Some breeds work better under the closer supervision of people (Caucasian Ovcharka) whereas others are more independent (Akbash Dog); some breeds show moderate herding behavior in addition to guarding (Polish Tatra, Cuvac) whereas most do not herd at all; some are more placid (Great Pyrenees), others more active (Kuvasz). The final choice of a protection dog will probably depend on activity level, your tastes for physical appearance, the cost and availability of puppies, the qualities of the breeder and guarantee offered, and your impressions of the litter's sire and dam.

Some of the early manuals on care and selection of livestock protection dogs insist that only young, newly weaned puppies can be bonded to sheep or other livestock. This is not necessarily so. Properly introduced and guided older pups can be successfully trained with livestock, although more work is usually required and such a dog may be less dependable in situations such as open-range grazing. Even mature companion dogs have been known to make the transition to livestock guardians, although this requires an experienced handler. Such dogs usually prefer to have closer contact with people.

COST

You should expect to pay from $400 to $1,000 for a puppy or young "started" dog. The details of payment will vary with each breeder; sale price usually does not include shipping costs. Some breeders prefer a certified check in advance, others will take payments, and some may entertain barter or trade as an additional option. These days, payment can be made electronically from bank to bank. This is especially useful when the breeder lives across the country or the ocean from you. Occasionally you may find a fully trained adult for sale, for which you should be prepared to pay considerably more if the dog is in good health and not too old.

Working dogs could be considered a commodity, like the sheep or poultry they protect. There are some breeders who produce livestock protection dogs in order to make a profit. Their main characteristics are lower prices, vague guarantees, usually oral, and broad assurances that their dogs will do anything well. However, there is an attractive alternative. Today there is a growing trend among some breeders to go in the opposite direction—to treat their dogs and breeding stock more humanely and to take extra care in using optimal rearing practices. Ethical breeders carefully evaluate each litter and match pups with appropriate buyers. They offer follow-up advice and training. They consider themselves part of a knowledge team that is working with you. The placement record of breeders who have put more effort into each pup will be more successful as a result. There is more work involved in this style of breeding, so they may also ask more money for their pups. Any additional expense will probably be worthwhile for you. We have heard of livestock protection dog pups being sold from the backs of trucks at livestock auctions for as low as $100—no guarantees, preferably no questions asked, and certainly nothing in writing. Is this a bargain for you? The initial cost of a puppy is small compared to the amount you'll spend on veterinary visits, inoculations, dog food and maybe bringing your fencing up to standard. Consider what you are getting for what you are paying. We recommend that you consider the total package—breeder, guarantee, long-term support, the pup's genetic background, and probability of success—when you select a puppy. To learn more about the work and role of an ethical breeder, see Chapter Thirteen.

GUARANTEES

Any investment of more than $300 should include a guarantee. Insist on assurance that the puppy will remain healthy for at least two weeks from the time of shipping and ask for a written guarantee that the dog will not develop any major hereditary defects later in life. If possible, you should already be aware of the genetic defects which affect the breed under consideration. If not, it may be worthwhile to do more research by contacting breed clubs or checking books and websites which list congenital and heritable disorders of various breeds (see Bibliography.) You might also want to make sure the breeder is aware of these genetic diseases. Some breeders are not well informed, and others will deny there are any problems in their breed. The latter is simply not true, so you may wish to exercise caution with a breeder in denial—she may not be as knowledgeable as she should be about other aspects of her breed as well. Some breeders will insist on replacing a defective puppy; you may prefer to receive a cash refund. Ask if the breeder has already begun a vaccination program and what recommendations she has. You will also want to check with your own veterinarian about diseases in your area that the pup needs to be vaccinated for.

In fairness to breeders, do not expect a guarantee that each puppy sold will be free from all forms of defects. Perfect dogs do not come along very often, if at all. Genetics is an imperfect discipline of science, so breeders will not be able to precisely predict every aspect of their "product." Research indicates that a growing puppy's diet and lifestyle, factors that the owner controls, may contribute to the development of such disorders as hip dysplasia and osteochondrosis. (These disorders are discussed in greater detail in Chapter Eleven.) Therefore, a breeder cannot assume total responsibility for all potential problems. Some puppies will grow in awkward leaps and spurts. They may become ungainly and seem out of proportion at times, or even develop a temporary lameness during periods of rapid growth. Transient situations such as these are not defects in the dog. We believe that a written guarantee should accompany every puppy sold, but it must be worded in a manner that is fair to both the buyer and seller. For instance, a breeder may state that if the puppy is overfed and as a result grows too quickly, she will not guarantee the dog should he develop orthopedic diseases.

On the other hand, breeders have their share of responsibilities. Their

Healthy Kangal Dog pups raised in the United States. Photo by Sue Kocher.

breeding stock should be carefully selected, based upon behavioral and physical characteristics, radiographic evaluation of the hips and specific testing for any problems associated with the breed. If a breeder becomes defensive or evasive as you continue to talk about terms of a guarantee, look for another breeder.

Both common sense and research data suggest that some puppies, even those from the best working sires and dams, will not be successful guard dogs. There is likely to be a small number of failures in every breed of protection dog. To avoid the possibility of being set up with a "lemon," ask for a guarantee of performance, for instance, a guarantee which specifies that the dog will exhibit protective behavior by twenty-four months of age, provided that the pup is given a reasonable opportunity to develop in

SAMPLE BUYER'S AGREEMENT
AND SELLER'S GUARANTEE

Sky High Ranch, the seller, guarantees that the Livestock Protection Dog purchased by the buyer,_____, will be free of any major genetic defects and will have a protective temperament at maturity (24 to 36 months), providing that the buyer raises the dog in an appropriate environment. What the dog protects will depend on the manner in which the dog is raised and is the responsibility of the buyer upon consultation with the seller. A dog that fails to protect satisfactorily after appropriate training, or breeding stock with a serious genetic defect will be replaced or a refund will be offered (see details below).

The seller will provide a dog or puppy to the buyer in healthy condition with current vaccinations, and will guarantee good health for two weeks after the sale. The buyer is responsible for providing proper veterinary care, vaccinations and nutrition to the dog thereafter.

If a pup has not already been neutered or spayed at time of sale, the seller will refund $40 to the buyer who neuters the dog at an appropriate age, without having previously used the dog for breeding, and after submission of documentation by the veterinarian who performed the neutering. This will not apply to a purchase based on trade, reduced price, in the case of dogs neutered after two years of age or in certain cases of re-sale. The seller will register the dog with an association that recognizes and represents the Livestock Protection Dog.

The buyer agrees to have the hips of their dog radiographed by a veterinarian at two years of age. The radiograph must be submitted for evaluation and certification by PennHIP or to the Orthopedic Foundation for Animals (OFA) located in Columbia, Missouri, U.S.A. The buyer understands that this is not optional, and must be done within 6 months of the dog's second birthday. If the dog has been neutered or spayed, the seller will refund $80 to help with those expenses. In order to receive this refund, a spay/neuter certificate must accompany the radiograph results if the pup was not sold already spayed or neutered. A dog to be used in a breeding program must be OFA certified at the owner's expense.

It is not required, but highly recommended that non-breeding dogs have their eyes examined by a board certified ophthalmologist, and certified by the Canine Eye Registration Foundation (CERF). Such an exam is quick, does not require anesthesia and provides valuable breed information. Dogs to be used in a breeding program must have their eyes certified.

The seller will sell and register all dogs with non-breeding status, for a non-breeding quality price. A dog that is sold for breeding purposes will be required to have OFA certification, eyes passed with CERF, temperament testing at maturity in consultation with the seller, conformation assessed by the seller in person or via videotape and an upgrade fee paid to the seller as previously agreed upon by the buyer and seller. When these conditions are met, the seller will re-register the dog with breeding status.

The buyer agrees to only breed their Livestock Protection Dog to another purebred Livestock Protection Dog of the same breed. The buyer will not breed Livestock Protection Dogs that have genetic problems such as hip dysplasia. Any pups born showing serious problems or deviations from the breed standard will be destroyed or neutered and not used for breeding.

The buyer agrees to use discretion in placing his/her pups or adults should he/she decide to breed Livestock Protection Dogs. This is a working breed and must be placed with people who realize that this is a large, guard dog breed that requires space and firm handling. Buyers will preferably have previous experience with other large guard dog breeds. Livestock Protection Dogs should be placed where they will be able to use their working ability. This is not an appropriate breed for those who just want a docile, loving companion. Companion dog owners must provide safe fencing for their dog when he is left unattended out of doors, to protect the dog from injury to himself and innocent people and animals outside the owner's property. Livestock Protection Dogs tend to have a large sense of territory and must be safely controlled at all times.

The buyer agrees not to sell nor to give away a Livestock Protection Dog to any individual or organizational representative who is not willing to enter into an AGREEMENT similar to this one. Prior to relocating a dog, the buyer will inform the seller and give them the first option to take the dog. The buyer should also be willing to guarantee any dogs that he/she places.

The **buyer** agrees to notify the seller of any serious problems with the dog that may be inherited or have a heritable component. These include osteochondrosis (OCD), hormonal imbalances, susceptibility to skin conditions, gastric torsion, autoimmune disorders, etc.

The **buyer** must notify the seller of any physical or temperamental problems as soon as they become apparent in order to be eligible for a future replacement or refund. A dog that has been overfed and deemed overweight by a veterinarian any time prior to three years of age will not be guaranteed against any orthopedic defects, including hip dysplasia.

Causes for replacement of neutered/spayed, non-breeding dogs that have not been overfed, supplemented or inappropriately exercised: hip dysplasia resulting in clinical symptoms that require corrective surgery; extreme shyness; no protective behavior (when appropriate).

Causes for replacement or partial refund of dogs represented as potential breeding quality: same conditions as above; or an OFA rating below Fair; heritable eye diseases such as retinal atrophy or non-traumatic entropion; distinctly overshot or undershot bite; undescended testicle(s); sterility unrelated to accident or disease; shyness. The **seller** will decide whether to offer a replacement dog or a partial refund so the purchase price is reduced to that of a non-breeding dog. A buyer may decide if they do not wish to take a replacement dog.

Other disorders or problems not mentioned in the above lists that result in surgery, ongoing medical expenses and/or seriously compromise the dog's quality of life and/or ability to guard may also be considered causes for replacement.

Replacement shall be made as soon as possible upon receipt of documentation from a licensed veterinarian that the defective animal has been spayed or castrated. The **buyer** is responsible for all veterinary expenses and the cost of shipping the replacement puppy. In the event of any type of corrective surgery for hip dysplasia, entropion, etc., the seller must be notified immediately upon diagnosis and reserves the right to request a second opinion from a veterinarian not associated with the first, review radiographs and confer with other veterinarians **before** any surgery is performed. If the above conditions are not met, the seller assumes no responsibility for providing a replacement.

Refund of purchase price is justified if a dog must be euthanized or dies naturally within the first two years of life due to disease acquired at Sky High Ranch or an inherited condition, as documented by a licensed veterinarian, and the buyer does not wish to take a replacement dog.

Buyer's Signature

_____

Buyer's Name and Address (print or type)

_____

_____

Phone_____   Date _____

_____
(signature)
Joe Shepherd
SKY HIGH RANCH
Wild Creek, MT 12345
909-123-4567

a healthy, conducive environment. A guarantee can't specify what the dog will guard; that depends on the owner and the working environment and, hence, is out of the breeder's control. You should be able to obtain this type of guarantee from any established breeder who is in business for the long haul. Keep in mind, though, that dogs that come with excellent working pedigrees, good health records and guarantees will cost more than puppies from a pet owner or a farmer whose bitch was bred by accident.

LOCATING A BREEDER

Where can you locate a breeder of livestock protection dogs? Your best source of information may be a satisfied local owner. Ask him about his experiences with his dog and the breeder from whom he purchased his animal. If he was satisfied with the arrangement, he should be happy to provide you with the breeder's name and address. You might also want to check your local paper for advertisements for livestock guardian breeds. Your agricultural extension agent or veterinarian may also be a source of information. Ask if they know any local owners or breeders who are using their dogs for working purposes.

Don't become discouraged if you can't find a dog locally. Ads for dogs can often be found in livestock trade journals. Magazines such as the AKC Gazette, Dogs in Canada, Dog Fancy, Dogs Annual and Dog World regularly carry advertisements for puppies. Don't overlook national breed clubs. Most publish newsletters which keep owners up-to-date on health information and other items of interest. They may also feature advertisements for puppies and older dogs. If you have doubts about the club's focus, request back issues of the newsletters. The articles, pictures and letters to the editor will reveal the club's practices and let you know if there are owners who specialize in working protection dogs. At first glance, a breed club may not seem terribly important. However, if you are inexperienced with training techniques or specific health concerns and features of a breed, the club may be a valuable source of information. You'll benefit from the articles in the newsletter and learn of other owners who can help you if need be. Many clubs now have branches and committees which deal exclusively with the issues of livestock protection.

Finally, there is a plethora of information on all breeds and breeders available via the internet. Most breed clubs will have their own web pages that include breed and breeder information. There are several e-mail lists which deal specifically with livestock protection breeds, and non breed-specific web sites. These are excellent resources for those who are electronically connected.

Don't be afraid to buy from a breeder who lives too far away for you to easily reach. Domestic and international airlines generally provide safe transportation for animals. Experienced breeders are quite capable of arranging for a puppy—or even an adult dog—to be flown to you or sent via ground transport. Shipping costs will be yours, but they are not likely to increase the cost of purchase more than ten to fifteen percent. If you don't own a shipping crate, the breeder can buy one for you and it will be yours to keep when the dog arrives. Some airlines will ship COD, but the pup and crate should be prepaid. Be prepared to forward a cash advance to the breeder to pay for the crate and the freight cost. The crate becomes a

A fine litter of Akbash Dog pups. Photo by Diane Spisak.

home for the puppy during transit and can be used as a sleeping station for the puppy at your farm or home, at least until it is outgrown. If you already own a shipping crate of the appropriate size, consider sending it to the breeder. Breeders often place a crate without its door in the puppy pen for two or three weeks before weaning and shipping. The pups become comfortable by playing around the crate and even sleeping in it. This procedure reduces the trauma of air freight and helps to make the crate a handy sleeping place for the young dog when he arrives at your home.

When looking for a pup to protect your livestock, you should focus on litters from working sires and dams. Puppies from show dogs who live exclusively in a home or kennel may lack the instincts needed for protection duty. There can be reasonable exceptions. Some breeders will keep a breeding dog as a house pet instead of as a livestock protector, especially if

Happy owners Willeke and Huub Hendrix hold their puppy, Zeki, and a Shetland lamb. The family travelled from the Netherlands to Canada to meet the breeders and bring their new family member home. The lamb stayed behind. Photo by Nick Hendrix.

they already have adequate protection for their livestock, or if the dog serves as a family and home guardian. Breeders may wish to have a dog that is well socialized so visitors can approach the dog safely for a closer, hands-on inspection. However, even a house dog should still show guardian abilities, and ideally the dog has already proven himself with livestock before coming to the house. In the home situation, this protection would be directed toward people or the house, instead of animals. In this instance, it would be acceptable to consider puppies from a "non-working" dam or sire. On the other hand, be suspicious of so-called working puppies if the breeder has no livestock, neither of the parents protects livestock or the parents were not imported from a country where they or their parents were working dogs, or if show championships and pedigrees are mentioned as a key selling point. Very few protection dogs will excel in both livestock protection and the show

Wally, a nine-week-old Komondor pup. Photo by Lyn Bingham.

ring. If you are in doubt about the working ability of a litter, ask for references of previously placed puppies from the same parentage.

Here is a simple test that you may wish to use to decide if breeders are being completely honest about their puppies. Assuming you have been talking to a breeder about purchasing a working puppy, ask a friend to call the same breeder to ask about purchasing a show dog. Ask your friend to sound as enthusiastic and credible as possible, and to inquire about delivery dates, costs, pedigrees and backgrounds as if he really wants a dog. Then compare notes. Is the breeder describing the same litter with a completely different emphasis to each of you? Do you get the impression that the breeder knows a lot more about the show circuit than livestock protection? If so, move on to another breeder. You will have invested the cost of a few long distance phone calls and saved hundreds of dollars that might have been spent on a less-than-desirable puppy.

A breeder's knowledge of her breed's characteristics, the strengths and weaknesses of her breeding stock, and your specific needs in a puppy are essential if she is to make a good recommendation for you. Unless she is gifted in mind reading, she will necessarily have some questions. If a breeder is more interested in talking about how cute the pups are than in learning about your needs and farming situation, be suspicious. Make sure the breeding parents have the health clearances required for that breed and that the breeder is knowledgeable about the breed and is selecting the best pup for you.

You should expect to be quizzed by the breeder. A reputable breeder will want to know about your own experience with dogs, your expectations for a livestock guardian, what your situation is (space, livestock, fencing, other dogs, other handlers), whether you are looking for breeding or non-breeding quality, working or companion dog. Sometimes these questions may seem rather personal, but she should have the best interests of her pups in mind, and should want to make sure you will be getting the right breed and right puppy. She will be the person you will be calling for advice later on, so she will also want to make sure you are as well informed about the breed as possible. A good breeder should be willing to send you information about the breed and her particular dogs. If you end up buying one of her puppies, you may be entering into a long-term relationship with this breeder as long as your dog is alive and with you, and perhaps even beyond. Of course, there are breeders who, once the pup is sold, would just as soon not hear from you again. Such breeders generally are only interested in the money they can make, and are best avoided.

SELECTING *YOUR* PUPPY

Once you have narrowed your selection of breeds and breeders, you will have to consider individual puppies within litters. Many breeders will insist on selecting a puppy for you, or guiding you in your selection. This is generally good advice—the breeder should be most familiar with the individual pups, should have interviewed you thoroughly so she understands exactly what you are looking for, and is therefore in the optimum position to recommend which pup would best suit your needs. Ask if the breeder has used a puppy aptitude test (PAT) to evaluate the litter (see Chapter Eight). This test is administered by a stranger, not the breeder, to the pups, and is a useful tool in determining the aptitudes and behavioral tendencies in pups of around seven weeks of age. If you live close enough to visit the breeder, you may be able to test the pups yourself, with the breeder's permission.

If possible, observe the pups interacting with each other. Watch them individually. You will likely observe some pups that are very active, others that are less so; some that will come running to you, others that keep their distance. People who want their dog to guard small stock such as sheep and poultry or who live on small acreages may not want the most active pups. These pups can get bored more easily, which may result in harmful play

Eight-week-old Slovakian Cuvac pup already started with sheep. Photo by Robin Rigg.

behavior directed toward the stock. On the other hand, a rancher with hundreds of acres to patrol can benefit from a high-energy dog. If you are looking for a companion dog, you may wish to avoid the pup that hangs back and does not seem particularly interested in you. Pups that are hungry or have just awakened from a nap may not be as active as when they are fully awake, so be aware of those cycles. If pups seem unusually lethargic, they may be ill.

Then consider physical traits. Just as newborn human babies are sometimes covered with short-lived dark hair, so we have seen newborn puppies of white-coated breeds variably colored at birth. By twelve to sixteen weeks of age, the coat will change to adult coloration. Therefore, don't be suspicious of improper breeding or advertising if a breeder of white dogs shows you puppies that have markings somewhat different from the parents. If you are uncertain, ask for a guarantee that the dog you buy will meet color standards. Pigmentation of nose, lips and eyerims on white dogs especially may be another factor to consider. Breeding quality dogs should have appropriate pigmentation for the breed. For dogs that will live outdoors, particularly at high altitudes and in sunny climates, dark nose, eye and lip pigmentation should be a requirement to protect them from sunburn and skin problems such as cancer.

Conformation is another consideration for dogs that will be required to work for a living, covering a lot of ground during patrols. Be familiar with what constitutes sound conformation by reading the standard for the breed. Be certain that the parents have had their hips certified free of hip dysplasia. The conformation you observe in an eight-week-old pup will be indicative of his adult structure, so be critical. For instance, a pup that never trots or one that seems unable to stand still periodically may have structural problems that don't allow him to do so. (see Bibliography.) Size can also affect the soundness and physical stability. We firmly believe that bigger is not always better, although most people tend to be impressed with the upper extremes in height and weight of livestock protection dogs. Many of the tallest and heaviest dogs are beleaguered by orthopedic problems, and are often less agile and less sound than the smaller ones.

Finally, you must consider the question of sex—male or female? If this is your first puppy, or the only working dog you will have, sex may not be relevant if you do not already have a preference. There does seem to be agreement, however, that most males will take longer to mature and settle into trustworthy guardians. This means more commitment of time on your part to observe and train before you know for sure that he can be left alone with the stock. Also, more males than females will display dominance aggression towards owners, although one can argue that this is rarely a problem with dogs that are raised properly in the first place.

If, however, the pup is your second protection dog and will be expected to work with an older dog, or if you already have a house dog that may interact occasionally with your working dog, you are best advised to pick the opposite sex. In other words, if you already have a female, select a male puppy for your second dog. Two females together tend to be the worst combination. If they are not compatible upon maturation, their battles can be deadly, whether they are intact or spayed. The next worst combination is two males. If that is your only option, it is best to neuter the males. Females should also be spayed if they must work together. Estrous cycles can disrupt normally congenial relations regardless of the combination of sexes. Same sexes can work together if they are compatible and have plenty of room for maneuvering and lots of work to do. Unfortunately, we have not figured out a way to reliably predict which dogs will be compatible with others, except to suggest that when dogs must be combined, opposite sexes tend to work better. Matching dominant dogs with more submissive dogs when possible is also a good idea.

The Puppy Arrives

Whether you are at home, at the breeder's or at an airline freight office, chores and obligations begin when the puppy is first handed to you. Start with any immediate needs the puppy may have. He may be soiled from a rough trip, hungry and thirsty, cold or hot, and disoriented in his new surroundings. Check the physical condition of the puppy carefully. If the pup appears overheated or thirsty, give him a small amount of cool water immediately, and let him rest a while before offering any food. If the trip has not been too long, you may want to wait until you have arrived home before feeding him. Please remember the breeder when you arrive home, especially if the pup has had a long trip. She has invested eight to ten weeks of intensive care in the puppy, not to mention many months or years of planning. A telephone call to say the puppy has arrived safely is always appreciated. If the puppy is not behaving as you think he should or if you are concerned about the health of your pup, please let the breeder know immediately. If you have any questions about the health of your pup, a checkup by your veterinarian may be worthwhile for your peace of mind.

Equally as important as the physical comforts of your pup are his emotional needs. You begin to develop a relationship with him as soon as you have made eye contact, spoken to him and touched him. In order to have a successful working relationship with your dog, you must develop his trust in you. Providing food, water and a safe environment are just part of the equation.

It was previously believed that pups should not be touched at all lest they bond to the humans and not to the stock. In fact, such dogs can be dangerous if they cannot be handled when they have to be moved, dewormed, groomed or even have their nails clipped. All ranch dogs occasionally have to see a veterinarian.

You can begin with a series of exercises called "sensitivity training." Gently roll the puppy on to his side and praise him when he relaxes. Pick up each paw, lift his ears, open his mouth and stroke him all over from nose to tail. Make sure you feel all his joints, and run your hands along the back legs from top to bottom. Some dogs, particularly maturing males, become sensitive about any handling near their genitals or the rear if they have not been exposed to it as pups. Eventually you will need to trim his nails, clean his ears and give oral medication. If you handle the pup daily and gradually introduce nail clippers, a cotton ball inside the outer ear flap and fingers inside the mouth, he will not mind so much when you or a veterinarian must do this later, even if he is injured and in pain.

You should also be able to lift your pup off the ground by cradling your hands under his chest (see Puppy Aptitude Testing in Chapter Eight). This should be a gentle, quiet movement with soothing words, lasting for a few seconds or until he has relaxed. Always praise him as you set him back down. When he is too large to lift, you can put one arm around his shoulder and the other under his chest and just lift his front feet off the ground. He should be praised for not resisting. These exercises teach your pup that

Maremma pups and lamb growing up together. Photo by Jay Lorenz.

you are in charge without handling him in a rough or threatening manner. They are not meant for older dogs who have not been treated this way from early puppyhood.

Take the pup on short car or truck rides while he is young. The same principle applies as above—teaching a malleable, young, 20-pound puppy and getting him used to something new is so much easier than doing the same with a 100-pound dog, especially in an emergency situation. You should try to expose your pup to anything you expect him to encounter later on. Do this in controlled manners, creating positive experiences for him. This way, your dog will not become alarmed by rides, movement of the sheep, visits by strangers, oral inspections, ear cleaning, nail trimming, new sounds, or whatever.

INTRODUCING AND BONDING
YOUR PUPPY TO LIVESTOCK

As soon as the puppy arrives, it's time to begin the training that will eventually create a superb guardian of livestock. One of the more important aspects of training is to create the correct environment for a process called bonding, or as some prefer to call it, grafting. Bonding is the development of a close identification between animals, or between an animal and a human. The phrase "a feeling of kinship" denotes a similar idea. When the puppy has grown into an adult, he will guard whatever he likes or identifies with, or, in other words, whatever he has bonded with. The best time to start the bonding process is as soon as possible after the puppy is weaned. This is not to say that a dog will fail as a guardian if the bonding process is not started before the puppy reaches three or four months of age. The program described is intended to maximize the chances of your dog successfully bonding to your livestock.

An ideal place to keep your new puppy is in the barn or some other protected location near the livestock. To start off, it is usually best to place the pup in a secure pen next to the livestock where he can see the animals he will eventually be expected to live with and protect. The pen should be large enough for him to exercise and play in. Provide a few dog-proof toys to play with to provide him some diversion and exercise, such as rope toys or large fresh bones. If you choose to keep the puppy in an outdoor pen or pasture, provide a shelter from the elements. The advantages of keeping a pup separated from the stock are that the dog cannot injure a lamb, a ewe

Akbash Pup playfully paws a lamb. Innocent behavior if that's where it stops, but without supervision this can escalate into chewing on ears and chasing. Photo by Diane Spisak.

A mature friendly ewe is ideal to keep with young pups. Photo by Diane Spisak.

cannot injure the puppy, and the puppy can be fed without having to protect the food from livestock. On the other hand, the chief disadvantage is
that the puppy is more likely to become bored and may try harder to
escape.

Whenever you are at the barn or doing chores, let the puppy out so
you can supervise him and protect him from aggressive animals. This way
the livestock will gradually become accustomed to the pup and he will
learn appropriate behavior around them—what is tolerated by the stock
and by you. This approach is particularly useful with older stock that are
initially fearful or suspicious of the pup, with very young or small animals
who could be easily hurt by a playful pup, or with a pup that is too rambunctious.

If the pup runs at or tries to bite the stock, he must be disciplined
immediately if the animals don't do it themselves. A quick and short correction is most effective, such as yelling "Aargh!" and interrupting his
behavior just as he is in the process of starting it. If a verbal correction is

Sadie, a five-month-old
Great Pyrenees and a
ten-day-old cria check
each other out while
mama llama oversees
the meeting. Photo by
Janice Reed.

insufficient to stop him, you may have to grab the pup by the scruff and lift him off the ground a few inches, in addition to your verbal disapproval. Do not shake him like a rag doll once he is off the ground. That may be effective discipline, but it can also result in spinal injuries. If lifting the pup does not work, and he resumes his aggressive play behavior, you may have to quickly grab the pup and pin him to the ground, still using your verbal reprimand. Release him when he submits to you by rolling over and breaking eye contact. Finally, if this has no effect, put the pup back into his pen and take him out another time, perhaps later in the day.

Be reasonable with the amount of force used to stop bad behavior, but do stop it. Teaching correct behavior now is much easier than trying to retrain a dog that has developed bad habits. This is the time to learn exactly how much force you need to apply to achieve submissive displays from the pup and prevent him from repeating the misbehavior. The degree of physical force necessary to be assertive with a three-month-old pup is much less than with a pup six months or older, so now is the time to establish a leadership role with the pup. For more details on subordination exercises, see Chapter Nine.

An ideal situation which allows for the bonding of pup to livestock is to leave him with older animals, such as a couple of wethers or ewes, that are unafraid and tolerant of pups, but will not put up with rough play behavior and can discipline the pup without injuring him. You can leave the pup with these animals in their own pen for several weeks until you feel he will be safe with the rest of the flock. If such animals are not available, you will have to continue to supervise until the pup no longer attempts to play with the stock.

When the puppy is behaving reasonably around the livestock, not trying to chase or bite whenever you turn your back, you can begin to leave him with the flock for short periods of time. During this transition you will want to be sure he is trustworthy. One way to do this is to spy on the pup when he doesn't know you are watching. This can take quite a while in some cases, and not everyone is able to devote that time. However, it is very important to know if the pup is ready to be left alone, since this is the most common training problem with young livestock protection dogs—owners trust them with livestock before they are actually ready for that responsibility. Young pups often go through a phase of being perfect angels until they grow as large or larger than the livestock, at which time they may resume attempts to engage the stock in play. Then you will need to resume supervision and discipline as necessary.

An Anatolian Shepherd Dog pup rolls over submissively in front of a curious ewe. Photo by Jay Lorenz.

Although most pups enjoy any attention from people, resist the urge to pick up and cuddle the cute little puppy for hours on end. If you spend too much time playing with your puppy, he will bond to you to the exclusion of livestock. People are much more interesting than livestock, so most dogs will seek the companionship of humans over animals. Don't bring the cute little bundle of fuzz into your home so the children (or you) can play with him for long periods. No damage will be done to livestock bonding if members of your family play with the puppy for a few minutes a day at the barn or if he comes to the house once in a while for short visits. The dog should not, however, become too emotionally dependent upon humans. Place the dog pen in a location that is out of sight of the farm house, preferably out of hearing range as well. You will want the puppy to like you and look forward to your visits, but he must have lots of opportunity to discover and bond to the livestock. The other side of the barn, away from the activities of the house, is the ideal place to begin training a livestock protection dog.

BOUNDARY TRAINING

Most people will expect their adult guardian to remain within fenced boundaries. Even ranchers whose dogs patrol hundreds of unfenced acres will want their dogs to stay in smaller pens or pastures from time to time. For this reason, it is well worth your while to train a very young pup to respect the boundaries you have set for him. A pup that learns early on that it is impossible to escape, or that it may be painful to even try, will be much more likely to respect fences, gates and walls later on. One of the leading causes of death and trauma in young livestock protection dogs is being hit by motor vehicles after leaving their pastures or properties. Owners of companion dogs must be even more vigilant at keeping their dogs at home because they usually live closer to busy roads and potentially fatal traffic. Owners in rural areas often have a false sense of security, not realizing these dogs can easily travel miles from home to explore or patrol what they consider is their territory.

The best way to boundary train a young pup is to make sure he is never successful at escaping from the enclosure you leave him in. It helps if he is content and does not wish to escape; however, most pups, no matter how entertained they may be, will eventually be curious about the world outside the boundaries and will make some effort to explore it. Livestock protection dogs possess keen senses of smell, vision and hearing so they are well aware that a lot is happening beyond their reach. In other words, you can expect them to challenge the boundaries.

A very young puppy can usually be contained with chain link, small grid woven wire, solid wood or metal fences and gates. However, they are capable of squeezing through small openings, or if the earth is soft, enlarging holes and digging out. Some pups will learn to climb woven wire or chain link fences. Older pups and dogs can jump if the fence is low enough, although we find many don't choose that route, preferring to go through or under a barrier. When a pup is motivated, you will be surprised at how clever he can be in devising a way to escape enclosures. Owners must be even more devious in preventing those escapes. If tight fencing is inadequate, and you find yourself contemplating having to bury fencing two feet into the ground to stop a digger or spending hundreds of dollars to replace all the fences, there is still one more type of fencing at your disposal—electric.

In case you are not familiar with electric fences, they are electrified wires which, when touched, give a shock. They sound a lot worse than they are. Commonly used to contain livestock, electric fencing is inexpensive, highly effective and easy to install and maintain. "Hot" wires carry a high voltage but a very low amperage. This combination can be felt, but will not normally do any harm. Fence chargers are electrical transformers with two terminals. One terminal is connected to a ground stake that has been driven into the earth. The other is the "feed" line which is connected to wires that have been insulated from the ground, usually by plastic holders. Electric fences give a shock whenever a dog or person (or another non-insulated object) connects the "hot" wire and the ground. The better the connection, the larger the jolt of electricity delivered. If you receive a mild shock from a fence charger while standing on dry gravel, wearing rubber boots, your dog will receive a stronger shock from the same unit. This is because his foot pads are usually moist, enabling him to make a better connection with the ground.

Depending on their strength, fence chargers may produce a tingle, a jolt, or a painful shock. We don't recommend the powerful units designed to service miles of cattle fences, unless that is the nature of your operation. Smaller chargers are more economical, often battery-powered, and don't pack as much punch. They can be purchased from most feed and fencing stores. The principle advantage of an electric fence is that it lets a dog know, in absolute terms, the exact boundary of his domain. Once he learns he cannot escape from a smaller pen or pasture, a dog is not likely to challenge any fence. Puppies we have trained with electric fences have shown respect for all fences they've been put behind for many years after.

Stringing one hot wire just above the ground where a pup might dig, another one a few inches above if he is inclined to squeeze through a square of woven wire, and one toward the top of the fence if he is a climber or jumper should be enough to discourage just about any escape artist. You must not forget the gates. We line our metal tube gates with chicken wire, then string one hot wire on the inside of the pen. This wire can be detached with an insulated, spring-loaded handle when we need to open the gate. Our main sheep pasture is a six-strand electric fence, which, once they are trained to it, is never breached by the dogs or sheep.

We have heard of many creative fencing solutions, but by far the most reliable way to train dogs to stay in is with electric fencing. Even if you cannot hot wire all of your pastures, you can do so for a smaller puppy training area and you will thus establish respect for fenced boundaries.

An alternative or additional type of electric fencing is the radio or invisible fence system. The dog wears a collar that acts as a receiver. An insulated wire cable is buried or laid around the boundary of the fence.

Invisible (radio) fence wire (arrow) reinforces the woven wire fence. While the wire could be buried for cosmetic reasons, on this farm the wired is stapled high enough on fence posts to be out of the way of weed cutters and lawn mowers. Photo by David Sims.

When the dog approaches within a few feet of the cable (you can set the distance), the collar emits a beep. If the dog continues to approach the cable, he will receive a shock. Although these systems can be used without physical barriers, we recommend that they be used where a fence or other barrier already exists to reinforce the boundary. We use this type of fence primarily in the winter around the barnyard since drifting snow often buries our regular fences. Radio fencing prevents one of our keenest escape-artist/coyote-hunters from digging under regular fences where we do not use electric wires.

Prices for these systems are reasonable, especially considering the investment you are making in your puppy. However, radio-fencing may not be economical for larger farms and ranches. Another caveat is that dogs must wear the collar in order to receive the boundary signal, and this requires that its two metal prongs (smooth, not sharp) be in contact with the skin. Cheap units may not be safe and have been known to cause burns, but even the better products may cause chafing if the collar is too tight or not removed periodically.

THE NEW PUPPY AND OTHER DOGS

If you have other working or house dogs, your puppy should be introduced to them one at a time. Your protection pup should know all the dogs and people that live and work on your farm. Be certain that they are introduced repeatedly during the puppy's development. An ideal situation is to raise a puppy with an older, established guardian that is tolerant of the pup and will engage the pup in play. If the puppy is alone, he will still need an outlet for his youthful energy, so he may be allowed to play with your other dogs, but only for short periods and away from livestock. You should avoid playing with other dogs in sight of your protection dog as this may incite jealousy.

If you use herding dogs, you will need to train your pup to ignore the herding dog when you are working the sheep. Your objective is to raise a livestock protection dog that will tolerate the actions of herding dogs only in your presence. If the same herding dogs or strange dogs were to run your sheep when you are not present, you would expect your protection dog to interfere and defend your flock. Puppies are excellent mimics—they learn by watching and repeating observed behavior. You don't want a livestock protection dog to learn to eye, chase, nip and control the sheep. One obvious solution is to remove the livestock protection pup from the flock while the herding dogs are at work. However, this may not always be practical or desirable. You can chain the pup to a fence post while the herding dog is working, and reprimand the pup anytime he shows interest in what the herding dog is doing. Use verbal disapproval if this works, or if you are at a distance you can throw a noisy object toward the pup (such as a soda can filled with rocks) without hitting him. Eventually he should learn to ignore the working herding dog and not try to join in. Most pups raised with herding dogs will accept them and not try to emulate them if discouraged early on. Older dogs not accustomed to herding dogs may not accept them and may have to be restrained while the herding dog is doing his job. This could also be the case if strange herding dogs are brought onto the property to work your stock. Introducing a herding dog into the mix creates what we call a human-animal-animal-animal interaction. This is more complex than simply working with sheep and a protection dog, and perhaps this is not for everyone to try. On the other hand, the use of herding and protection dogs concurrently is commonplace throughout the world. If you have a need for simultaneous use of both kinds of dogs, and this is almost always when shepherds are constantly with the flock, pay attention to the learning cues of your protection dog pups, and you'll succeed.

Raising more than one livestock protection pup at a time has both advantages and disadvantages. One advantage is that the pups have each other to play with and use up their youthful energy. Ideally, they will direct all the normal chasing, mouthing and biting behavior towards each other and not the sheep. If they are in a situation where predators are common, they will eventually turn their attention to patrolling. We know a rancher who successfully raises groups of pups together and then puts them out on range with adults. There the pups have supervision both from shepherds and from mature dogs, and lots of work to do—an ideal situation. In a less than ideal scenario, say where space is much more restricted, raising two pups together may help overcome the frustration of boredom. Boredom invariably leads to problem behaviors such as destructive chewing, digging, excessive barking, chasing stock and escaping when possible.

The disadvantage of raising pups together is that they may bond more strongly to each other than to the livestock or the owner. In many situations this is not a problem since dogs often protect stock by simply being territorial—bonding to livestock is not always necessary. However, two pups together may eventually "pack up" and direct their play behavior towards the sheep; they may require more supervision than one pup alone. There are also two pups to train at the same time, and most people barely have enough time to train one properly. They should be taught their commands separately—not many people have the skills to train two pups at one time. Finally, it is a good idea to separate the pups periodically and give each one time away from the other so they do not become too emotionally dependent on each other. Whether such rearing is successful or not will very much depend on the management of the pups and the stock, the physical setup, time available for training and, to some extent, the genetic makeup of the pups. We do not recommend more than one pup the first time you raise a livestock protection dog. Once the first dog is trained, you have the advantage of that experience when training the second one. In addition, the older dog will do a lot of the work for you, helping train the second pup and providing an outlet for play.

CHEWING

The growing protection puppy will engage in many of the playful games that all young dogs exhibit. Between three and five months of age, the permanent teeth will begin to appear. During this period the puppy will be inclined to bite and chew quite hard. You should provide toys for the pup, including objects that can be safely chewed such as large, indestructible balls, rope toys and large bones. If such items are not available, he will find things on his own to chew and destroy—wooden mangers, posts, barn siding and rocks come to mind. We went through many garden hoses learning this lesson. We have also heard of dogs hospitalized for chewing and swallowing inappropriate items, like plastic bottles and bags.

One problem that has to be dealt with quickly is the mouthing and biting of livestock. If a puppy starts to chew on lambs or begins pulling wool, a natural extension of playing instincts normally directed towards other puppies, he must be corrected immediately. The timing of your corrections is critical. Make certain that the puppy knows you do not approve

Provide safe toys to entertain your pup while she is alone and to give her something to mouth and chew. Score: one for Winnie the Akbash, one for the megaball. Photo by Bob Montgomery.

of chewing on lambs by using a harsh voice to interrupt his behavior as soon as it begins, or just before. You will quickly learn to recognize the signs of a puppy about to start a play-chase sequence: the way he may crouch, do a play-bow, cock his ears or lower his head. If he does not respond to a verbal reprimand, you may have to use a more direct physical approach such as hitting the ground near him or slapping the pup on the rear with something like a riding crop. If you are too far away, you can throw a can with pebbles to startle him. If that is insufficient, and some pups can be difficult to deter, you may have to grab him by the scruff while growling harshly at him, making an "Aargh!" sound. A particularly determined pup can be grabbed by the scruff and jerked to the ground while you growl and stare at him; then immediately release him. If he does not stop his behavior once you have let him go, or if he resumes shortly thereafter, you will have to repeat the correction more forcefully or remove him from the lambs/kids and not allow him to interact with them unless you are present to supervise. All corrections should be short, only a few seconds long. Once the pup stops what he was doing and averts his eyes, rolls over or yelps, stop the discipline.

Another suggestion is to apply a bad tasting liquid to whatever the pup is chewing, such as lambs' ears, to discourage biting. A product such as Bitter Apple, Boundary or Chew Guard can be quite effective. However, chew deterrents need to be reapplied.

If you take care of this rather predictable problem behavior early on, biting won't become a habit. We repeat, this is one of the most common mistakes new owners make—trusting their pups with livestock far too early. Please don't forget to reward appropriate behavior. There are so many ways you can signal your approval of quiet, respectful behavior around the sheep. Think about this, and reward your pup the way he most appreciates.

Many people are amused to have a little puppy chewing on their arm or undoing shoe laces. To many owners, there does not appear to be any harm in this play activity, but there is. In the case of livestock protection dogs that may end up weighing 140 pounds, that "harmless" play can grow into a serious problem. The dog is learning that mouthing people is acceptable behavior. You will no longer find it acceptable in a few months, so avoid the problem in the first place by letting the pup know when he has applied too much pressure with his teeth. For sensitive pups, withdrawal of attention can be an effective way to communicate your displeasure. By ceasing to play with them, puppies teach their littermates that they have gone too far. If this is not effective or the pup does not associate isolation with his biting activity, you will have to be more direct. This can be done by vocalizing with an "Ouch!" or "Aargh!" and removing the arm. If the pup resumes biting, repeat the vocalizing. Some pups are so intent on biting, treating it like a game, that you will need a much stronger deterrent. If he continues to bite, give him a surprise squirt of lemon juice in the mouth or nose. The small, plastic, lemon-shaped containers are perfect for this technique. You can hide the lemon in your pocket and take it out quickly when the pup goes into a play-frenzy of biting. You may want to practice your aim before actually using it on the pup. For truly resistant dogs who are determined to shred your shirt or your arm, a squirt in the eyes may be required. Lemon juice will sting but should cause no long term harm. The only time pups should ever be allowed to play roughly using their teeth is with other "consenting" dogs.

FEEDING YOUR PUPPY

The diet you choose for your puppy is important. We will briefly mention diet here and will devote a full chapter to the subject later on. The breeds of dogs that are usually used for livestock protection are large and are therefore most susceptible to bone and joint problems. Research on one disease, osteochondritis dissecans (OCD), suggests that leaving puppies with unlimited amounts of food is not a good idea. Animals that are not nutritionally pushed to grow as fast as they possibly can are less likely to develop bone and joint problems. Additionally, dogs kept in lean condition all their lives can live up to fifteen percent longer than overfed dogs and are not as likely to suffer from elevated blood pressure, diabetes, or heart and liver problems.

Here is a routine that gives a puppy as much food as he needs: Offer a high-quality food twice each day, at whatever times fit your schedule. At the end of five to ten minutes, take the food away. Be aware, though, that if you stay around during this time, the puppy may be less likely to eat if he wants to play with you. Leave the puppy alone during feeding times. The actual amounts of food to offer a puppy will be described in Chapter Ten. The objective is not to feed the puppy to satiation; he should still want to eat slightly more than what you have offered him. While we realize some may not agree, our recommendation is to switch from a high-quality puppy ration to a high-quality adult chow any time after three months of age (despite what the advertisements say). However, if you do not feed a premium dry dog food or raw food, stick with the puppy chow for a full year. Pups should also have access to fresh, raw bones to chew on when possible. Make sure the bones are not cooked and are large enough they can't be swallowed. We will discuss the use of raw foods in Chapter Ten. Fresh water should be available to a pup at all times unless he is being raised in the home, in which case it may be withdrawn in the evening to aid in house-training.

BASIC TRAINING

Large dog breeds tend to mature more slowly than the smaller breeds you may be more familiar with. Young puppies may put on amusing acts of guardianship for you, such as a warning bark when you first walk in the barn, but they should not be expected to really protect livestock for at least a year. Some become protectors by six to nine months, but others may take eighteen to twenty-four months or more to mature and find their places. As with other breeds, these dogs go through playful puppyhoods and goofy adolescences.

One of the best lessons you can teach a new dog is to walk beside you, on leash, as you patrol the perimeter of the property that the dog will be guarding. Loop the leash through your belt or around your waist to keep your hands free. Then, if you bring the dog on leash as you do your chores, filling water troughs, pitching hay and feeding the animals, the livestock will be more likely to accept the new stranger and the dog will learn that you care about the animals.

In terms of traditional obedience training, your eventual goal is to have a dog walk with you on lead, sit, come, stop and perhaps lie down on command. That is about all you will need in the way of commands with a protection dog, although this may not be so easy to accomplish. Learning to sit for treats is not usually a problem, but teaching a livestock guardian to come consistently is one of the more difficult exercises. Begin working on these basic skills as soon as your puppy arrives on the farm. Some owners of working livestock guardian pups will take them to public obedience classes, not so much to teach their pups the commands, but to socialize them away from the farm. Although this is something not all would wish to do nor can do, taking your pup off-farm to meet with other dogs does not seem to affect his ability to discriminate between strange dogs intruding on your property and those he meets away from the farm in non-threatening situations. Initially some believed that friendly exposure to other dogs would ruin a working dog. In fact, we have seen many dogs who can be fearsome guard dogs on their own turf, but when taken off their properties, can be reasonably well-behaved in the presence of strange dogs. There will be more information on socializing and training the companion dog in Chapter Nine.

As with other breeds of dogs, yours may be sensitive to harshness. Some puppies are easily disciplined. The first hint of you being upset with him will have the puppy crying for forgiveness. At the opposite end of the sensitivity spectrum are pups that seem to require strong physical corrections to deter them from inappropriate behaviors. Most pups will fall in between the two extremes. Occasional harsh scoldings, especially if warranted, should not damage a pup's self-confidence, but you need to learn the tolerances of the puppy as soon as possible. If a pup continues a misbehavior after being disciplined, your actions were not effective. You need to increase the strength of correction, use a different method or improve your timing. If your timing is off, he may not associate your correction with the misdeed.

Whatever their level of sensitivity, all pups should learn to tolerate handling and touching all over their bodies from early on. As mentioned earlier, at some point you will need to trim toenails, remove a burr from the coat, check ears or mouth for infection or treat a wound. If the pup has not become accustomed to this level of handling when he is young, you may be in for a losing struggle with a 100-pound dog that resists. For more details on puppy training, establishing a leadership position and controlling the puppy, refer to Chapter Nine.

The basics of puppy care include proper shelter, adequate food and water, location of the pen such that the puppy will be encouraged to bond to livestock, protection of both the puppy and the livestock from each other, isolation of the puppy from other dogs if necessary, adequate exercise and socialization, and training in basic commands. Following this regimen may not be easy; however, the guarding instincts of the puppy will likely be strong enough to overcome a few excesses or errors. The dog will most likely work even if you have not followed these instructions to the letter. Your puppy will be able to live comfortably in the conditions that we have described above for several months. During this time, study the behavior of your puppy, get to know his personality, and be prepared to adjust the instructions in this book or other sources to meet the needs of your situation.

Top: Three-month-old Akbash Dog pup Ruya uses a ewe for a pillow.
Bottom: Submissive licking. Photos by Orysia Dawydiak.

The Adolescent Dog

During the fourth through twentieth months of his life, your dog will undergo major changes in size, maturity and, possibly, temperament. Behavioral problems ignored during puppyhood will be more difficult to correct now, but can certainly be managed. This chapter has been divided into sections dealing with the more common problems encountered with an adolescent protection dog.

By four or five months of age, your dog will be too large and restless for containment in a small pen. You will have been taking him for controlled on-leash walks around the perimeter of your property (whether or not there are fences along that perimeter), and the puppy will be familiar with the commands "stop," "sit" and "come." You may want to begin leaving the dog with your livestock for variable lengths of time, keeping in mind one very important consideration. A livestock protection dog may not begin to actually guard until he is somewhere between one and three years of age. Protective behavior intensifies as the pup matures, although it may seem to appear suddenly one day. It is a slow, gradual process, so be patient.

You will have to put the dog out with the livestock to complete the bonding process and to teach him which areas of property he should protect. During these months, at least periodic supervision is required. If you must leave the dog unsupervised for more than a day at a time, you will want to devise a method of making food available to him in such a manner that sheep or other livestock cannot eat it. Utilizing a corner of a pasture, place a series of two or three bars horizontally across the corner and nail up an old sheet of plywood to act as a roof. A pan of dog food will be accessible to the dog, which can easily crawl under the bottom bar. Sheep will have a much harder time crawling under, and will probably not learn to do so if the dog becomes at all territorial about his feeding station. Another idea is to train the dog to eat from a feeder that requires pushing open a lid. Some dogs will adapt to this plan well, but others won't. Livestock, especially goats, may also learn to operate the feeder. During adolescence most protection dogs learn to guard their food from livestock. They will not usually hurt livestock investigating the dog food but will chase them away from the food bowl.

OVERACTIVE DOGS AND ESCAPE ARTISTS

Adolescent dog behavior is highly variable. Some young dogs seem to spend most of their waking hours trying to figure out new ways to escape from the pasture while others will show no inclination to leave even the most poorly fenced enclosures. Some dogs will be considerate of the livestock from the first day they meet, yet others will chase and try to play with them. Sentry duty can be rather boring, especially when nothing much is happening and there are no predators to warn off. A young, growing dog will naturally want to exercise and play. You must discourage any play that results in harm to the livestock. Most owners are unable to watch their dogs constantly during this period yet still wish to keep the dog with the stock. For such occasions they can use a drag or dangler to limit the playful activities of their adolescents. Before describing this method, we must emphasize that this should only be considered a temporary solution and does not actually teach the dog not to chase.

A drag is a piece of wood, a tire or any other item that is not sharp or dangerous, that can be attached to the dog's collar by a length of chain. Dogs usually adjust to them fairly quickly. A drag will slow down a dog that wants to play and chase livestock. It will also interfere with any attempts to escape through, under or over fences. You can prepare three or four drags, and use the one that is most appropriate for specific situations. Drags are easily constructed from fireplace-sized pieces of wood, say, twelve inches long. A small one is three inches in diameter and a large one can be fourteen inches in diameter. A drag can be up to one-quarter the weight of the dog. One or two fencing staples are driven into an end of the wood. Then a short piece of stout chain is used to attach the log to the collar. Openable C-links can be purchased at a hardware store to connect log to chain and chain to collar.

The length of a drag chain is critical. If you want to slow a play-chasing dog, make the chain short, say three feet, so the log or other weight

Recipe for a dangler or drag: one piece of wood, a
heavy staple, two C-links, a length of chain.
Drawing by Orysia Dawydiak.

trips the rear legs. The dog will be able to get around by learning to walk
slowly and a bit sideways. If escaping is the problem, use a longer chain.
Chances are the dog will catch the chain or log on the fence as he tries to
crawl under or jump over. Make sure the chain is long enough that if the
dog climbs or jumps over, he can land on the ground with the drag still on
the other side of the fence, to avoid being strangled in midair.

A variation on the short drag is a dangler. This is essentially the same
item, but with a very short chain. A lighter piece of wood is attached to a
six to ten-inch length of chain, so that it strikes the dog's chest and front
legs during rapid movement. A dangler can slow a dog considerably without involving a large weight. On the other hand, it may not present as effective a deterrent to escaping as a regular drag does.

A drag may be used as a substitute for the mature protection dogs and
shepherds who would control the behavior of younger dogs in an "old
world" setting. Drags do not look nice, but the dog soon learns to make life
easier for himself by walking slowly around the livestock or by staying in
the pasture. If a coyote or other intruder ever enters the field, the dog can

A small log acts as a drag to keep this bitch from leaving the pastures. Photo by David Sims.

still move very quickly when he is so motivated. Fast motion is harder, though, so a dog is less likely to engage in play while a drag is on. The instances when we have seen a dog in full motion while wearing a drag have been when he perceived a threat to his flock of sheep. If you are concerned that the dog may hang himself up on the drag while going over a fence or wall, remain in the area when you first put it on to observe or check on him. The only instance of a fatality resulting from the use of a drag that we are aware of occurred inside a barn where the drag was too short. A drag should not be used inside a barn since there are too many places where it can catch. Another possible problem with drags and danglers is that dogs may injure themselves if they do choose to run by bruising their legs or perhaps straining their necks and shoulders. Drags and danglers should not be left on dogs for long periods of time.

In addition, never leave anything attached to a choke collar, or leave a choke collar on a dog that is free. In fact, we believe choke collars are never appropriate, even for training purposes.

One word of self-defense is warranted: If you ever come home later than usual and head out to feed a very hungry dog wearing a drag, be careful that you don't get wrapped up in the chain and taken for a ride across the pasture. Dogs rarely keep track of their own tails, let alone a drag with you attached. Danglers can also be bruisers of thighs and knees.

Another temporary solution to the chasing/biting/wool-pulling dilemma is a basket muzzle. If it is properly sized and fitted, this type of muzzle allows a dog to breathe and lap water, but not to bite. It can be put on the dog if the owner must leave him in with the stock but is worried he may chase and nip at the sheep in his absence. Again, it does not teach the pup that biting is inappropriate behavior, nor does it prevent him from chasing the stock if he is bored.

SOCIALIZATION

Socialization of your protection dog is an important topic, worth discussing again. In particular, an intact male may become very protective as he enters puberty. A lovable puppy could transform into a fierce, growling dog

An adolescent Maremma shows submissive behavior when challenged by a ram. Notice the legs lifting to expose the belly, the half-closed eyes. Photo by Jay Lorenz.

A young Anatolian Shepherd tolerates the attentions of a spirited miniature horse colt. Photo by Henry Ballester.

if you have not taken steps to socialize him and establish yourself as being in charge. One partial solution is to neuter the dog. If you want to have an intact dog, be prepared for sudden challenges to the pecking order. Your dog may become unfriendly to livestock that wander near the food bowl, even if it is empty, or he may even challenge you. Be prepared for continual challenges to your authority as he matures.

Livestock protection dogs are big and they usually are not as well socialized as house dogs. Be aware of situations in which a stranger may unintentionally act aggressively and is likely to be bitten. For example, fence lines are often guarded more fiercely than other portions of the dog's territory. Do not encourage visitors to put their hands through a fence to pet a dog that has demonstrated aggressive behavior. We have observed that dogs are more likely to feel threatened by a hand poked through a fence than by a person who walks into their field. A direct stare by a stranger can also elicit an aggressive response, so visitors should be warned to avoid direct eye contact.

Most livestock protection dogs are calm, loving creatures around their owners and the livestock they live with. However, be prepared for

This ten-month-old Caucasian Ovcharka is still in training, shown here with the entire team of shepherd and herding dog. Photo by Robin Rigg.

changes in behavior which may occur during maturation, or when a bitch comes into heat. Lactating bitches and bitches in season may display a higher level of aggression towards livestock and people, even those they know. If a protection dog has never seen children before, you cannot assume that he will recognize them as small humans. Children often are less inhibited than adults, move less predictably, make higher-pitched noises and may be addressed in a different tone of voice than are adults. Protection dogs may perceive that children are threats to the livestock and may respond aggressively. For this reason it is essential that young pups and dogs be exposed to a wide variety of ages and types of people as they are growing up. (See Chapters Seven and Nine for socializing with children.)

POSTING SIGNS

One last word while on the subject of safety around dogs: Put up one or more signs indicating that you have a dog on duty on your premises. A sign is a warning that may save you from a liability suit should a person be bitten on your property. In addition, overzealous people have been known to shoot dogs seen in with sheep in other farmers' fields. A sign may save your dog's life, by informing others that a dog is supposed to be with the livestock. Such a sign might read, "Livestock Protection Dog on Duty—Please Do Not Disturb."

A posted sign can protect your dogs and the public. Photo by Brooks Parrott.

SEXUAL DEVELOPMENT

Sometime around six to seven months of age, sexual development will begin in earnest. Decide in advance what you are going to do with a bitch that is in heat. You will need a dog-proof kennel, one that will keep her inside and any lusting males out. Estrous cycles can last for two or three weeks even though she is only fertile for about three of those days. This will be a time when you cannot expect the bitch to be an effective protection dog. She will have other things on her mind, as will any intact males nearby. Similarly, intact male protection dogs can be distracted from their duties by the enticing smells of a bitch in heat. Both are more likely to wander if not contained adequately.

Neutered protection dogs will eat less food, remain healthier (lower incidence of prostate problems) and offer considerably less hassle. Neutered dogs are as territorial as they need to be to effectively guard livestock, and are less likely to roam. Spayed females are also less likely to develop mammary gland tumors and other medical problems associated with reproduction. For these reasons, we recommend that you neuter or spay your protection dog. Some breeders are now having the procedure performed prior to shipping, since pups can be neutered safely at seven weeks of age. Advantages of early neutering include ease of handling smaller pups and a shorter recovery period, so you may want to learn if your veterinarian will do this for you.

PHYSICAL PROBLEMS

Larger breeds of dogs may be more prone to certain skeletal problems such as hip dysplasia. If afflicted, they also will suffer more due to their size and weight. There are visible signs that may indicate your dog is suffering from a bone or joint malady. Watch your dog as he moves, especially when he is not aware that you are looking. A dog that knows you are watching or that is eagerly approaching you for affection can suppress the pain that comes from an aching joint, bone or muscle. A dog is most likely to show signs of painful movement when he is getting up from sleep or rest or after a bout of vigorous exercise. If you consistently see these signs, consult your veterinarian. Orthopedic problems as well as other health issues are covered in more detail in Chapter Eleven.

CONTINUED TRAINING

Dogs like to receive human attention. An owner can easily make the mistake of paying more attention to a "disobedient" dog than to an acquiescent one. If you are a parent, this may sound like a familiar scenario. Thus, a dog might actually be encouraged by an unwitting owner to escape, chase livestock, howl at night, become a fussy eater or even become hostile to other people, because negative attention is more desirable to them than no attention at all. Similarly, a dog might react in these ways out of boredom, even if the owner is doing a fine job overall. We cannot write a formula that describes the appropriate amount of attention that a livestock protection dog should receive each day. Each person-dog combination will establish a unique relationship. An experienced dog handler can decide if the dog is clearly separating rewards and praises from words of punishment or disapproval. An inexperienced handler may need to consult a local professional or veteran amateur dog trainer for an evaluation of the strengths and weaknesses of his training program. At any rate, owners must work conscientiously to be certain that their dog knows why he is being punished or ignored, and why he is being praised. We admit that this is not always easy.

YOUR DOG'S SAFETY

From your perspective, your livestock protection puppy may be attractive and affectionate. However, if a dog-hating neighbor were to see the dog out with your flock and not realize he belongs to you, he might decide to do you a favor by shooting the pup. Deputy sheriffs have been known to shoot protection dogs, with the best interests of the farmer in mind. Many people will automatically assume that a dog in a pasture with livestock is a predator. On the other hand, if you publicize the presence of a new guardian puppy, you might worry that someone may try to steal him. The solution? You will have to decide what is the proper amount of publicity versus privacy for your situation, but in general it is a good idea to let neighbors know about your new pup and what his job will be. Unless your puppy is extremely well contained behind solid or electric fencing, he could escape. Hopefully your neighbors would recognize him and alert you or return him to you. Inviting your neighbors over to meet the pup would be worthwhile.

A young male Akbash Dog has found his ideal companions. Photo by Orysia
Dawydiak.

Permanent identification, such as a tattoo inside the ears or on the
flanks is advisable in case your pup should wander far away. Microchips are
also used to identify dogs, although it is not always easy to read them or
even to find someone with the correct equipment to do so.

One of the leading causes of death of young livestock protection
dogs is motor vehicle accidents. These breeds, like most others, simply do
not develop the ability to avoid cars and trucks; some will even chase
vehicles either on the inside of their fenced pastures or along the roads if
they are loose. Even in Turkey, where very little fencing is used for grazing livestock, the guard dogs often accompanied our vehicle as we drove
out of villages, biting at our tires as we tried to speed away without hitting any dogs. On your own property, in those few instances when you are
driving a hay truck or sheep trailer into a field where a guardian dog is

on duty, be especially careful. If you are going to be working the sheep, take the time to remove the dog. That way he is not so likely to be run over.

If any of your neighbors regularly sets poisoned meat out for coyotes, or uses traps or explosives to destroy varmints, you will want to be extra confident that your dog cannot access them. Some dogs can be taught to avoid bait stations and traps. If these predator control techniques are used in the vicinity of your sheep pastures, invest the time and trouble to take this precaution. It may also be worthwhile to try to convince your neighbors not to use these devices, many of which are highly restricted or no longer legal.

We conclude this chapter with a brief list of basic management considerations. Have you checked the dog's collar lately? As the dog grows, he will need to have his collar loosened or replaced. Have you started a file of the dog's medical records? Have you established a schedule for worming and vaccinating the dog? Are heartworms, fleas, ticks or foxtails a problem in your area? If so, take whatever corrective steps you and your veterinarian feel are required. If your terrain is rough, periodic inspections of the foot pads and undercoats of your dog are in order. Alternately, if your farm has soft, lush pastures, you may need to trim the dog's nails periodically, just as you trim the hooves of your livestock. Make a note to remember your livestock protection dog at income tax time. Our accountant recommends that a protection dog be depreciated as a straight line item over five years.

Adolescence is the stage of growth in which your dog is most likely to give you trouble. We predict that this will probably be the least satisfactory chapter for you because there will inevitably be problems and situations that are not covered. Don't be afraid to use your own imaginative methods to train your guardian dog. Be patient with him. Encourage and reward good behavior and don't take it for granted. There may be occasions when you doubt his ability, but most dogs do well, given time.

The Mature Dog

Somewhere between eighteen and thirty months of age, your dog will settle down to become the useful, dependable guardian that you hoped for. Protection dog maturation may seem to occur overnight or it may manifest itself over a period of months. You might find yourself remarking that the coyotes have not been howling like they did in previous winters. You might be calculating your livestock profits and notice that losses of young animals from predation are down. You may have never seen your dog do

This Abruzzese variety of the Italian Maremma shows the body posture of a relaxed, adult dog, head and tail down, as he patrols next to the flock. Photo by Agostino Molinelli.

anything useful, but the evidence will be in front of you—the sheep graze in quiet pastures and the dog has matured. Instead of bounding into the middle of the flock with head and tail raised, your dog is likely moving more slowly, patrolling the perimeter, with head and tail lowered. Your livestock may be choosing to bed down around the dog. They may be seen running toward the dog in response to a startling sound or smell. Your dog may be maintaining a guard post on the highest spot of easily available land.

By this time your dog will have developed his own personality. The livestock protection breeds are supposed to be independent thinkers. Words like aloof, stubborn or somewhat distant are often used when describing these dogs. For the most part, this is a time for you to relax, pat yourself on the back and consider that you did a good job raising the big fellow. However, there are still a few potential problems to be aware of, although the rate at which they may occur will diminish.

CARING FOR YOUR DOG

Remember your commitment to the dog's health. Maintain a regular schedule of treatment for internal and external parasites. Have you loosened or replaced the dog's collar as he has grown? Is he current on his rabies vaccination, which is usually required by law? There may be a booster annually or up to every three years, depending on where you live. The thinking on vaccinations for diseases such as distemper, parvovirus and parainfluenza has changed over the past decade. Rather than yearly boosters, current research suggests that a shot every three or more years is adequate to maintain titres of antibodies against these diseases. Some people are now deciding to only give puppy shots; some are giving no vaccinations at all and using alternative methods to boost immunity.

Veterinary visits can pose a potential problem for some dogs, especially those that have not been well socialized to strangers or that have rarely been taken on car rides. Such a visit can be traumatic. The fears that any dog could develop in a veterinary clinic may be far worse for a guardian dog. A terrified 25-pound dog can be held in your lap, but a 120-pound protection dog, accustomed to being the boss of his own territory, may present a problem for both you and the veterinarian. In reality, taking a protection dog to a veterinary clinic rarely presents a problem. We are intentionally overemphasizing a potential difficulty. In most cases, a protection dog when taken away from the farm no longer has anything to guard, is somewhat disoriented and will be calm and manageable.

Here are several suggestions to help overcome situations in which your dog may become aggressive in the presence of your veterinarian or other strangers. First, take your protection dog for rides every now and then. Do not leave your dog loose in the back of an uncovered truck, though. The rides need not be very far, but they will accustom the dog to travel. Second, keep your dog in your truck until the veterinarian is ready to receive you. In hot weather the waiting time should be kept to a minimum. Third, let the veterinarian and any veterinary assistants you meet in the halls of the clinic know that the dog has not been extensively socialized. A forewarned veterinarian and staff will be calm around the dog. These actions alone will probably prevent any traumatic situations. As the owner of a large dog, you have both moral and legal obligations to protect other people, yourself and your dog.

India, a Great Pyrenees, and her alpaca friend, Pi, both seek the shade of the same tree. Pi settles in next to India, who turns around and moves closer to Pi. Photo by Tawny Bott.

Should you require a farm visit by a veterinarian for some other reason, take advantage of the visit. Arrange for a rabies vaccination and a physical examination of the dog at the same time. To decrease the chance that your dog may feel territorial or threatened, have the vet see your dog outside of the sheep pasture.

HANDLING AGGRESSIVE DOGS

Some very aggressive protection dogs are truly excellent at their work. They can be handled by their owners and are gentle with livestock, but strange people cannot approach them without eliciting growls and aggression. If your dog is like this after you have taken steps to socialize the dog and had him neutered, you have probably done all you reasonably can to "tame" him. From then on your obligations are to post signs around the dog's field, keep the dog away from strange people, and protect veterinarians and others who need to come in contact with him. Dogs like this are less common than they used to be. The public should be forewarned about this dog's likely aggression, which is probably a result of incomplete socialization during puppyhood and adolescence. In our experience, the degree to which farmers socialize their livestock protection dogs varies greatly. Some strains within the protection breeds seem to be more timid or aggressive than others, suggesting that there is also a genetic factor involved. In general the most fearful dogs are the ones most likely to bite when stressed.

DIET FOR THE MATURE DOG

Livestock protection dogs will appear to be full grown by around eighteen months of age. They do, however, continue to "fill out" until the age of thirty-six months or more. Keep this in mind if you compare your dog to the breed standard and when you determine feed rations. Mature dogs require fewer calories per unit of body weight than do pups. If you have not switched from a puppy chow to an adult food by this time, do so now. Mature dogs do not need the higher calories found in puppy chows. Be prepared for variations in the amount of food your dog requires. Some factors which will alter your dog's appetite include extremes of heat and cold, the presence of new packs of dogs or coyotes (necessitating more patrolling or fighting), a move onto more difficult terrain, and pregnancy or lactation.

A Kangal Dog sharing shade with a few sheep and shepherds. Notice the matching black muzzles on dog and sheep. Photo by Elisabeth von Buchwaldt.

When selecting a place to put food and water for your dog, look for a location that is convenient for you and sheltered from the elements. Ideally this location offers a good view of the flock so that the dog can eat, drink and rest while remaining on duty. Some farmers put dog food on a hay wagon or under an idle combine, places a dog can hop or crawl into but sheep cannot reach. Whether you leave food periodically or visit the dog regularly will depend on your own circumstances; however, discrete meals should be fed when possible. A high-quality dog food should be stored in a cool, dry place since exposure to the elements decreases food value and may even cause it to spoil. By feeding your dog daily you will know that he is eating properly and you can check on your stock at the same time. This is simply good management practice.

CHANGING THE DOG'S ROUTINE

There will doubtless be times when you choose to modify the herd or flock that the dog is guarding. This may occur at weaning, when the lambs are shipped to market or when introducing new stock. Such an upset in the dog's environment may spark abnormal behavior, such as attempts at escaping or aggression towards the new animals. Be prepared to haul out the chain and drag if necessary. Keep in mind that new livestock may also need time to become accustomed to the presence of a protection dog. The dog may accept a new flock of sheep immediately, but the new sheep may be terrified by the sight and smell of a dog. New livestock may attempt to eat the dog's food due to greater than usual hunger incurred during transportation. Also, the rules of the pasture have not yet been established for them. This is another good reason not to leave the dog's food lying about.

Occasionally, a well-behaved protection dog will suddenly begin to harass certain sheep in the flock. In most cases we have found that those sheep differed from the others in some way. Examples include sheep that were ill and acting abnormally or that had bells attached to their collars. The dog sees them as strangers that don't belong. If your dog is used to all-white sheep, he may decide that the new gray sheep you brought in do not belong with the rest of the flock, and he will try to chase them off or at least keep them away from his regular flock. If this happens, revert to the leash and walk technique. Walk the dog near the new sheep as they are being fed a desirable foodstuff such as grain or alfalfa. Allow the sheep and dog an opportunity to become accustomed to each other while praising the dog for appropriate behavior. We have also noticed that new sheep are frequently pushed around by both adult rams and established ewes. When the protection dog sees them being bullied by the other sheep, he may decide to join in. If this behavior persists, the problem is best corrected by removing the dog until the sheep have re-established their pecking order.

Similarly, you may need to move the dog to a new pasture or range. When this occurs, walk the dog around the perimeter of the new pasture, on lead if need be, once or twice. This routine will establish a link between you and the boundary. The dog is less likely to leave a place that he associates with you. A drag may be indicated if the dog shows a reluctance to accept new fence lines. An old trick that may work with troublesome escapers is to mark the limits of a field or range with your urine. This calls for several days preparation and a watering can, or periodic walks around the pasture. In theory, the dogs will identify with your territory and choose to remain within it. If they cover your markings with their own, you are on the right track.

LAMBING TIME

We have observed instances of young dogs "protecting" newborn lambs from their mothers. Older dogs have been known to do this as well with the first born in each lambing season. The dog hears the plaintive bleating of the newborn animal and sees the mother licking away the placental membranes. His own protective instincts become activated. Dogs may become confused at their first lambing, so do not be too harsh if this happens. Walk the dog away and allow the lamb and mother to get together, or pen them together for a day or two if you can. You may also need to pen the dog next to the ewes if you cannot supervise, especially if this is the first time the dog is exposed to lambing or even in the second season of lambing. If you are around for an actual lambing, put the dog on a leash and teach him to stay back during delivery. If the ewe allows the dog up close, watch that he does not interfere with the process and only takes the afterbirth once it has been completely expelled.

Numerous cases have been reported of lactating bitches accepting lambs on their teats. This acceptance demonstrates the strong maternal nature of these dogs. Even males have been known to mother newborn lambs, kids, calves, puppies and kittens, cleaning them or allowing nursing attempts.

CONTINUING EDUCATION

Can old dogs be taught new tricks? Or, more to the point, has your mature dog chosen to "forget" the basic commands, such as "wait," "sit" and "come?" A fully grown dog accustomed to independence may decide to ignore your commands. Time for a refresher course. Young adults are just older adolescents, still testing you to see if you really mean what you say. For tips on reinforcing commands, see Chapter Nine.

Maternal behavior in these bitches extends to lambs as well as their pups. Anatolian photo by Jay Lorenz; Akbash photo by Orysia Dawydiak.

Specific Behavioral Problems and Solutions

CHAPTER

7

In this chapter we deal with some of the more serious problems that owners of livestock protection dogs may encounter. Problems are most often the fault of the owner, not the dog. However, human nature being what it is, there will be the temptation to blame the dog, at least at the time of an infraction. Chronic escaping, harassment of livestock, biting, general disobedience, nuisance barking and ineffective guarding are among the problems that may be experienced. Corrective management techniques including use of the electric collar can help. This chapter is designed to provide an errant owner with a second chance....Do not interpret its inclusion as evidence that protection dogs are biters, livestock killers or chronic escapers. They are dogs and, in the final analysis, they will react to poor management or inadequate early rearing in the same ways that other breeds of dogs would.

The following questions may help to determine the reasons for a dog's disobedience. Understanding the cause of a problem is essential if you are going to solve it.

1. Have you clearly expressed your disapproval of this behavior? Are your corrections properly timed and administered with appropriate force?
2. Are you subsequently rewarding poor behavior by petting the dog when you feel sorry for him, having just disciplined him?
3. Are other members of the family undermining your efforts?
4. Is the dog ill, too hot, thirsty, hungry, bored or otherwise unable to obey you?
5. Is there a nearby bitch in heat, overly aggressive livestock or a troublesome neighbor that might be interfering with your dog? If you own a bitch, is she in season?

6. Are you in control? Is the dog adequately trained? Will he come, sit and stop when you command him to? Are you afraid of your dog?

Consider these basic questions first, then read the specific suggestions below.

ESCAPING

There are many reasons why dogs escape from a reasonably sized field or enclosure. Many escapes are the result of boredom (something more interesting is available outside the pen) or because escaping is relatively easy and rewarding. Less likely considerations include health problems, harassment by livestock or humans, hunger or thirst. Maybe he is leaving the pasture that you had in mind because he wants to protect another band of livestock elsewhere. Perhaps he is chasing off roving dogs on a daily basis. That is to say, maybe he is doing exactly what you want him to do. Maybe he escapes to eat the better food you offer the "house" dog on the front porch. Possibly your neighbor's bitch is in heat. In turn, your guardian bitch may be in heat and is succumbing to wanderlust.

Regardless of the reason, most dogs learn to escape because they were initially contained in leaky fences. Having been successful a few times, they will continually try to find "weak points" in any fence and will be a challenge to contain. By the time they mature into adults, they can squeeze through an eight-inch gap under a fence in a wash or a draw, through a pipe gate or sometimes even through a six-by-six inch woven wire square! If a dog gets into the habit of escaping by one route, you may be able to curb the behavior by reinforcing the fence at that one location. We use long tent stakes to hold the bottoms of fences down to the ground where adolescent dogs try to crawl under. In washes, T-posts or electric fence step poles staked eight inches apart will effectively block low spots yet allow water to pass through.

The most effective way to contain dogs is the use of electric and radio fences (Chapter Four). If you have a pasture or field that is not too close to the house, but can be seen from a window (a kitchen window is almost always best, it seems), put the dog into that pasture. Keep an eye on the dog, using binoculars, if necessary. If/when he begins to escape, you will have a better chance of catching him in the act, and you will be able to apply instant correction. For sensitive dogs verbal corrections may be adequate, but for others nothing short of an electrical shock will deter them from attempting to escape (see section on use of electric collars below). The electric collar can also be used at a distance, allowing for immediate, properly timed corrections.

Some farmers report only one escape route that bothers them—the driveway. Dogs that show no inclination to escape otherwise may run down

Mixed breed livestock guardians in a mountainous part of Romania. The danglers were placed on the pups to discourage them from leaving the flock in pursuit of wild animals. The danglers were left on these grown dogs, although the boards no longer serve their function. Photo by Robin Rigg.

Mikey, one of North America's earliest working Akbash Dogs in central Oregon. Unfortunately, this young male jumped out of his pasture in pursuit of a truck and was killed. He had shown no interest in vehicles until he watched a bitch he had bred being taken away in a pickup. Photo by Orysia Dawydiak.

driveways onto a road when the opportunity presents itself. A possible cause of this problem is the tendency of protection dogs to check out every change in their environment, including joggers, bicyclists or strange vehicles if their domain includes a roadside. For limited routes of escape such as this, you'll need to catch the dog by surprise and issue a strong correction. One method is to borrow a neighbor's bicycle and become the cyclist that is chased. Or ride as a passenger in a car that is strange to the dog; do whatever is needed to be at the scene of the infraction. When the dog runs down the driveway after the car, ask the driver to stop, get out and issue your surprise reprimand. If you're on a bicycle, stop and throw a can with pebbles at the dog to startle him and send him back home.

We had a male Akbash Dog who knew that a coyote den was situated across the highway from the farm. On one or two occasions when the gate to the field was left open accidentally, he dashed down the driveway, across the highway and off to investigate the den. We installed a radio fence across the driveway (see Chapter Four), trained him that it was dangerous to go anywhere near the area and he decided not to go in that direction again. In spite of best intentions, gates are left open from time to time and the results can be tragic.

AGGRESSION TOWARD LIVESTOCK

Pack Behavior

Inappropriate aggression can be simple or difficult to correct, depending on the cause. Let's start with aggression toward livestock, listing some of the more straight forward cures. Is your herding dog getting into the sheep field from time to time? Herding dogs are naturally aggressive toward stock. They can teach bad habits to protection dogs, especially if your dog has not been taught to ignore them (see Chapter Four). One protection dog plus one herding dog equals a pack of dogs. Dogs exhibit altered behavior in a pack situation where their instinctive killing behaviors are more easily elicited. Earlier we discussed the pros and cons of raising more than one protection dog puppy at a time in any one field or pen. At a certain age, pups raised together and without enough work to do or proper supervision could potentially begin to harass stock.

Play Behavior

The aggression you observe may be the end result of play activity. The dog may be chasing, pulling wool and biting as he romps around the field. This rough play translates into aggression in our eyes, but is only an extension of dog play from his point of view. If you are not around to watch for play behavior, use a drag or dangler or remove the dog from the flock—he is obviously not ready to be left alone with them yet.

Protecting Food

Does the protection dog only bite or attack livestock when they get near to or try to eat his food? Maybe the answer is that the dog food is too easily accessible to the sheep, or that you need to feed your dog one discrete meal a day and not leave any food behind. Trying to teach the dog to ignore stock that come too close to his food is not easy, nor is it advisable. Food is one of those resources which triggers strong responses in all animals. Because we control this resource for our dogs, we can expect them to tolerate our presence and not challenge us when we make food appear and disappear. But they naturally protect food from other species and potential "competitors." Bones especially can be points of contention. Dogs that won't defend a bowl of dry food may become ferocious around fresh meaty bones. You may or may not be able to feed raw bones to your working dogs in the field. We have one young male that needs a huge area clear of stock around his fresh bones, whereas our bitches only grumble if the sheep get within two feet or so. Then they may just pick up their bone and move to another spot to avoid confrontation. You will have to gauge each dog's reactions before deciding if food or bones should be offered in places accessible to livestock.

Hormones

Hormonal cycles in dogs can alter their behavior toward livestock. Bitches in heat may become short-tempered and less tolerant of stock, even towards lambs bouncing around them. Intact males around such bitches may also become possessive of the bitch and drive off any stock that come too close. A stud dog separated from a bitch in heat may become so frustrated that he will snap at livestock that approach too near. This can be fatal in the case of small animals like poultry or vulnerable ones such as emu pecking the ground near the dog. Sometimes the only solution is to remove him or her from the livestock until the cycle is over—another reason to spay or neuter working dogs.

Barrier Frustration/ Re-directed Aggression

Irritable behavior can occur at fence lines when there is an activity on the other side which the dog would like to participate in—such as driving off an intruder. In this situation the dog experiences something we call "barrier frustration." The dog's frustration may then be re-directed toward any stock standing too close to him. When he snaps at or bites another animal during this state of agitation, we call this "re-directed aggression." One

Georgie, an Akbash Dog who protected a herd of horses in Alberta, became distracted by a herding bitch in heat and began to leave the horses. He was neutered and returned to work. Photo by Orysia Dawydiak.

hopes that if the dog displays this type of aggression, the stock will learn to keep their distance from him during such episodes. This type of aggression is not easy to control and may be exacerbated when dogs with a high work drive are contained in small pens or pastures. They have little opportunity to exercise their ability to run off intruders and perform their duties. In such situations, relocating the dog may be the only solution by finding him a new job, a new location with more space or work to do, or different live-stock to guard.

Aggressive Stock

Male livestock may elicit defensive behavior in dogs. Some rams and bucks, and even ewes or does occasionally, can be very aggressive towards the guard dog. They may paw the dog, butt him, push him around, or jump on him while he is at rest or trying to sleep. Many dogs will put up with this behavior for quite some time before they begin to defend themselves. In severe cases, the dog will actually go on the offensive, attacking first when he sees the offender approach. Sometimes this will correct the undesirable behavior of the stock; other times it turns into an ongoing feud. This of course is not a healthy environment for the dog who is supposed to be protecting the stock, and he cannot be blamed for repelling the attacks. In such cases, the aggressive animals should be removed or perhaps even culled. If the animals are too valuable and the owner does not wish to remove them, he should remove the dog—no dog should be expected to tolerate such abuse and still perform his job.

Strange or New Livestock

We noticed that one of our protection dogs was aggressive toward strange sheep on our property. When we rented out pasture space, a neighbor's sheep would be in a field adjacent to ours, so our dog was separated from those sheep by only one line of fencing. He became highly agitated when the strange sheep got near "his" sheep. When one of those ewes ended up on our side of the fence, he kept her separated from our flock. This action was handy, allowing us to easily capture and return the errant sheep. If we were to introduce a new ewe or ram into the flock, this would not be likely to happen, though, because we would be there, supervising the addition and letting the dog know that all was well. If your protection dog suddenly becomes aggressive toward livestock, check to see if there is a strange animal in the flock or herd. Similarly, when you place the dog with a new herd or add new animals to the flock, stay with the protection dog for a while. Chances are that the new animals have not had experience with a livestock guardian. Further, they may be afraid of the dog and may try to run away or even attack him. These forms of behavior could lead to defensive retaliation by the dog.

Crowding

Some dogs, especially intact males, are sensitive to being crowded by livestock. This may occur in barn pens or when moving stock down narrow alleys or runways. Correcting the dog for this behavior, a form of self-defense, is not usually effective. When possible, it is best to avoid putting the dog in that situation, making sure he has enough room to maneuver.

Possessive Aggression

From time to time, dogs become possessive of inanimate objects such as water and food bowls, mangers, hay bales, salt blocks, and certain areas in the barn. This behavior can be exhibited by males or females. A typical scenario has a dog lying in a hay manger, having claimed it for a bed, growling at livestock who come to feed. The owner must let the dog know, however he can, that this is inappropriate behavior. The usual corrections can be used—verbal disapproval, a shaker can, a swat with a riding crop or a radio collar. Using a remote-controlled electric collar (see further down in this chapter) is not advised since the dog must make an association between the correction and the object he is guarding in order for the correction to be effective. He could just as easily associate the shock with the livestock, and become more aggressive toward them, or afraid of them. A radio collar can be used if you wish to keep the dog out of a manger so that the dog is warned and shocked if he comes too close to it. There are units which emit a signal from a central area and wires are not required. If a food bowl is being guarded, provide a livestock-free area to feed the dog, or just offer discrete meals and remove the bowl after each feeding.

AGGRESSION TOWARDS OTHER LIVESTOCK PROTECTION DOGS

Protecting Food

If you have more than one working dog with your livestock, there are occasions when they may get into fights with each other. One typical cause of such altercations is food—such as when there is a fresh bone to dispute, or at feeding time when one may decide to check out the other dog's dish. The owner can try to prevent fights by making sure each dog only eats from his own dish, perhaps by keeping the dogs well apart or teaching them to ignore the other guy in the first place. If bones become the source of contention, as in the case with livestock above, perhaps they will have to be removed or not given to the dogs in the first place.

Barrier Frustration/Compatibility Issues

Another typical scenario is fence-line frustration, also called barrier frustration and re-directed aggression. Barrier frustration occurs when dogs desperately want to get to the other side of the fence to chase off an intruder, for instance, but they are unable to and become quite agitated and frustrated. The aggression may be re-directed, one dog attacking the other in frustration. This happens more often than people realize, even between two dogs who usually get along quite peacefully. It probably occurs with higher frequency where dogs have small areas to patrol and guard. There is not much one can do about this problem except hope the fights are minor and self-limiting, or split up the dogs. Also, the owner should try to pair up the most compatible dogs possible (see the discussion in Chapter Three on mixing the sexes). Generally, opposite sexes are the most compatible, followed by two males together, preferably neutered, then two bitches, preferably spayed. Spaying and neutering does not guarantee there won't be battles, but it removes the destabilizing effect of hormonal cycles and testosterone-triggered attacks on young males.

Unstable Hierarchies

In cases where there is more than one dog in each field and when one of the dogs is removed for a short or long time for any reason, a skirmish can erupt when he is returned. Dogs need to re-establish their positions relative to each other from time to time. If the relationship between two dogs is tenuous, removing a dog and returning him can destabilize the hierarchy that existed. The battles that result can be minor or major. This varies greatly from pair to pair. Some will co-exist quite peacefully for months; then a fight will break out. In the worst-case scenario, there are dogs that simply will not tolerate particular individuals and will always have to be kept separate or placed elsewhere. We have heard a number of stories of dogs killing each other over disputes of unknown origin—even dogs who had lived together for years. This is not a common occurrence, but it does happen. The best you can do is to be aware of different personalities and changes in the dogs or the environment that may precipitate fights. Try to keep the most compatible dogs together.

AGGRESSION TOWARD HERDING DOGS

When properly introduced in a neutral area, and initially supervised, livestock protection dogs should be able to tolerate and ignore a working herding dog, even while remaining in the same field with them. Occasionally there are personality conflicts and the protection dog simply won't accept the herding dog. Other times, the protection dog is too dog-aggressive, especially if he wasn't raised with the herding dog; he will have to be tied up or removed from the area where sheep will be worked.

AGGRESSION TOWARD PEOPLE

Legal and Insurance Issues

Biting humans is a more serious and complicated matter. Unfortunately, whether or not the dog is really at fault does not seem to have much bearing in a court of law. A good insurance policy is advisable when you purchase a dog that could hurt people. Most states and provinces have traditionally allowed each dog "one bite;" that is, an owner would not likely be sued for large amounts of money should his dog bite someone if the owner had no reason to suspect that the dog was inclined to be a biter. After one person has been bitten, an onus is placed on the dog owner to minimize the chances of further aggressive interactions. Then, considerations such as negligence and reasonable care become pertinent.

In recent years this common law approach to dog bites has changed in many jurisdictions. As our society has become more urban, laws have been enacted which place responsibility for controlling animals on the owners at all times. Contact a lawyer to ask what laws are in effect for your area with regard to dog bites. Many insurance policies will only pay for damages resulting from an individual dog's first biting incident. You are on your own paying for damages incurred in subsequent biting incidents. This is one of the limitations frequently buried in the fine print on the backs of policies. Ask your insurance agent about this to learn how your policy works. If your dog has bitten someone, under circumstances that many people (not just you and your best friends) consider appropriate or forgivable, where the dog was clearly acting to defend himself or his livestock, you may not want to take any corrective actions with the dog. In these cases, maybe the posting of a few signs is all you will want to do.

Socialization

Let's discuss ways to avoid a bite situation, to reduce your liability should one occur, and to re-socialize a dog that has become too aggressive around people. Virtually every protection dog puppy will be friendly with people. However, if the dog has been left to mature in a remote field, seeing only the same one or two people for months at a time, he may not retain a universal love and trust of all humans. Decide how friendly you want your dog to be toward strangers, then work toward that goal.

Some owners do not want their dogs to be friendly to strangers, especially when the owners are not around. They might even encourage aggressive responses under specific conditions. If you wish to maintain an aggressive dog in a place where people might encounter him, post signs that clearly warn of the dog's presence. Hopefully, this will protect even unwelcome intruders and help to reduce your liabilities.

If you are present, and your dog has been socialized to visitors, he should respond in a neutral or friendly manner to unfamiliar people. Even if your dog has been well socialized, don't invite trouble by leaving the dog in your absence with a flock that is about to be herded through a foot bath, trimmed, sheared or injected by strangers. The presence of strangers, mixed with the bleating of nervous sheep, will almost certainly bring out the protective instincts of the dog.

Most guardian dog owners are not worried about human intruders. They want livestock protection from coyotes, bears or dog packs. For these situations, encourage friendly interaction between all strangers and the protection dog. You may wish to go out of your way to socialize your puppy, inviting people over continually to visit with the pup, then the adolescent, right on up through adulthood. Keep in mind, though, that even the best socialized protection dog should still act defensively toward unfriendly strangers, especially in your absence.

Children

Dogs may think of children as non-humans. If your dog has not been exposed to many children, he will not have any reason to associate children with "real" people (that is, grown-ups), any more than he would associate barn swallows or cats with adults. Think about it. Children act differently. Adults frequently use a different tone of voice to talk to children than they do with each other. Children are smaller than adults and do not always approach and pet a dog the way an adult does. A child is as likely to pull fur or poke an eye as he is to properly pet an animal; therefore, your dog may associate children with pain. If, when a child walks up to a protection dog, the dog tucks his tail or growls softly, take note—the dog is confused or scared. If you live alone, or only with other adults, be careful when company with children arrives. They will likely want to pet your livestock protection dog. Chances are the dog won't mind, but watch the dog when the children are near him. Bitches in heat and dogs around bitches in heat are the worst offenders. Their minds are "elsewhere" and they are less tolerant, so definitely keep children away from them. Even if your dog has been raised around your children, it doesn't mean he will be safe with visiting children unless he has been socialized with them also. For details on socializing dogs with children, refer to Chapter Nine.

Dominance Aggression

Chapter Nine deals with socializing puppies and how to establish a healthy leadership position with your dog. Owners who practice subordination exercises with their growing pups should never be threatened by adult dogs, although most dogs will challenge owners from time to time, even in minor ways. If this relationship has not been well established, there could be serious challenges to the owner's authority as the dog matures. These challenges can take the form of not responding to commands, growling at the owner or even biting him. Strangers who try to assert themselves over such dogs may also end up being challenged and possibly bitten. This type of behavior is usually referred to as "dominance aggression."

If the owner is actually afraid of his dog, the dog will be aware that he has the "upper hand." Correcting this situation may be very difficult. Disciplining such a dog often results in escalating aggression and is not recommended. What should you do to re-train a dog that is showing unreasonable aggression to you or other people, and has become a liability to you? Situations of this nature need to be carefully analyzed on an individual basis. The dog may have to be kept in a place where he will have no opportunity to bite. Our recommendation is that you consult an experienced trainer or behaviorist. Although there are books dedicated to this subject, they will probably not suffice if your training of the dog has failed to the point where you have this sort of problem.

This less than pleasant subject must be concluded with the same qualifier we used at the beginning of the chapter—livestock protection

The young couple was desperate for advice. Their livestock protection dog was eight months old and was growling at the children and the wife, especially if anyone got near the food bowl. They finally faced up to the problem — they were afraid of their own dog, even though he could be really sweet at times. The breeder had told them that livestock protection dogs were creatures of instinct and required no special training. Besides, their dog looked kind of like a large, white version of a labrador retriever, so they didn't think they needed to do much to raise the dog to be a faithful, gentle companion.

Czar is a Caucasian Ovcharka with a medium level of aggression. Many of these dogs are considered to be too people-aggressive and/or requiring too much human attention to be left unattended with flocks. Photo by Thunder Hawk Caucasians.

dogs are, in general, gentle, loving dogs with their owners and familiar livestock. Still, they must have an aggressive component to their nature in order to be effective against legitimate intruders. We have provided this discussion of the biting dog just in case you need assistance, not because we think you will. We have talked with many livestock protection dog owners and are pleasantly amazed at the low incidence of bitings reported. When you decide to purchase a large guardian breed of dog, you must give thought to proper socialization, fencing and management. If your dog is raised with firm, fair and consistent handling, and properly socialized, you should not have to worry much about your dog biting or harming people.

The llama is giving Dutchess the Komondor a thorough examination, which Dutchess tolerates very well. Photo by Tawny Bott.

THE LIVESTOCK PROTECTION DOG THAT WON'T PROTECT

We have heard of many instances where protection dogs lie around all day, seem to sleep twenty hours out of each twenty-four, basically ignore the livestock and show a preference for life on the front porch of the farm house. When these events occur, many farmers conclude that their dogs are not working out. (If the dog really is lying on the front porch of the farm house, it could hardly be the dog's fault, anyway.) But then we ask the question, "How many lambs have you lost so far this season?" The answer is often, "Well, none, come to think of it." Another case has been solved—the dog works at night, the people get their restful sleep and the livestock are safer than they were without the dog. The only remaining step is to give the dog his due credit.

There are some protection dogs that make quite a show of their work. They patrol fields on a regular schedule, sniffing livestock, marking corner posts, barking, posturing and generally keeping themselves active. Most protection dogs, however, do not engage in this kind of busy work. Instead they conserve energy and your dog food bill. Unless you live in hilly or

In Turkey the dogs, like this Kangal Dog, usually have shepherds nearby to monitor their behavior. Photo by Elisabeth von Buchwaldt.

forested terrain, these "lazy" dogs probably work just as well as the "busybodies." There are reasons for this: a) the dog could well be active at night, when he is most required, but when you are least likely to watch; b) a large part of guarding is just being there, having dog odors available for other dogs and coyotes to smell; and c) there simply may not be much for the dog to do if all the predators shifted their attention to other farms and food sources soon after you purchased the dog.

Most cases of dog "failure" have actually been instances of dog success. There are, in fact, few true failures among protection dogs that have been adequately trained in the first place. If you suspect that your dog isn't doing his job, gather together the evidence. One dead lamb, or the occasional dead lamb, even lambs that have been obviously killed by coyotes, won't be significant, if lamb losses have been reduced from several each night to one or two per month or season. If you continue to have lamb losses, although they are admittedly reduced, maybe you need more dogs to cover your uneven terrain. Are your sheep of a non-flocking breed? If so, they will be more difficult to protect. Consider the age of your dog. Livestock protection dogs look large and imposing by twelve months, but they may not be physically and mentally mature until three years of age or older. Your dog may be working, but not yet at peak capacity. If lamb losses start up after a period of time when the dog was apparently doing an excellent job, examine the dog carefully for injuries. Ask if a neighbor has a bitch in heat or some other distraction for your protection dog.

Still, there may seem to be instances where a dog shows no inclination to guard. If a dog is completely healthy, is not being distracted by playful children or a bitch in heat, was not bullied by the sheep during puppyhood, was raised in a manner that should bond the dog to the livestock, and came from lines of proven guardians, then he should work. A person with a "non-guarding" protection dog would at this point want to reaffirm all of those prerequisites, and then have a good long talk with the breeder of the dog. In cases where the bloodlines, the early training and the management techniques of the owner were adequate, it would appear that a non-guarding dog was a true "dud."

The U.S.D.A. research bulletins on use of livestock protection dogs mention that there is a failure rate of individual dogs even among those that had all of the prerequisites for success. Yet, it has been our experience, and that of the Hampshire College Guard Dog Project, that a high percentage of those apparent failures work out fine if they are put in a new situation, with a new owner. We have sold dogs that we have seen guarding prior to leaving our farm. The new owners appear to be earnest and well-intentioned, but within weeks or months the dogs may fail to work for them. These apparently unworkable dogs would, however, become wonderful assets to new owners. In other words, the failures we have experienced have not been with the dog, but with the person-dog team. That is not to say that the people involved were overtly negligent. Rather, for complex reasons which often include inexperience and overly high expectations, or a poor match of dog with the stock and management conditions, they did not establish a good relationship with the dog.

If you are experiencing problems with your protection dog and are coming to the conclusion that the dog simply is not guarding effectively, you should contact the breeder and any other experienced people you know. If their suggestions don't help, maybe they will be able to arrange a swap of dogs between you and another farmer with a similar problem. A fresh start might be best for you, the other owner and the dogs. Breed associations, breed rescue groups and individual breeders may help to find a new home for a dog. Locating a new home or a suitable swap requires judgement, time and many telephone calls. Be prepared to pay for this assistance.

USE OF AN ELECTRIC COLLAR FOR SERIOUS PROBLEMS

The use of electric collars is controversial, especially with the current popularity of all positive reinforcement training. We do not advocate the use of shock to train dogs to perform obedience commands, for instance, but only when all other methods have been exhausted and the behavior is potentially dangerous to the dog or livestock. For those who believe shock training is cruel, it is not an appropriate tool. Shock training is usually less "painful" than the shock from an electric fence. The collar can be tested on your bare arm if you wish to know how it feels—typically it is not unlike a static shock you might get when you've removed your wool sweater and touched a metal door knob on a dry winter day.

Electric collar corrections are appropriate when you have tried all other available training methods but you still have a serious problem, such as chasing stock, which can be solved by long distance corrections. Electric collars have built-in batteries and electrodes. A person can push a button on a handheld activator giving the dog an electric shock from as far away as five hundred feet or more. The more expensive collars offer shocks of variable intensity or duration, and a buzzer or warning tone. Using the shock as a form of instant correction, you can teach a dog, very quickly, that specific behaviors are unacceptable. An electric collar may appear to be a dream come true. It can be useful, yes, but it has to be used with great care. Corrections must be timed precisely when the dog is about to begin the chase or is engaged in the chase; the shock must be associated with the activity you wish to interrupt and stop.

We shall summarize the steps involved with electric collar training. However, we recommend that you talk to an experienced user before trying one for the first time. You may be able to borrow or rent a collar from a breeder or trainer, and at least one company sells refurbished collars. There are many electric collars sitting unused, gathering dust. They were used for specific problems; once the problems had been solved, there was no further need for them. For more information on this method, you may wish to read Understanding Electronic Dog-Training, by Daniel Tortora (see Bibliography.)

The collar, with the electrodes, battery, buzzer and remote sensor, is larger and heavier than an average dog collar. Therefore, if the collar is put on and training begun immediately, the dog would quickly associate the collar with the shocks. The lessons would be lost when the dog did not have the collar on. To get around this problem, first place a "dummy" collar on the dog. The dummy looks just like the shock collar, having the same weight and metal box attached, but it can't create a buzz or shock. Put this on the dog for at least ten days before beginning corrective training. Several days before the actual training is to begin, carefully read the instructions that accompany the collar. Charge the batteries and keep the equipment out of the dog's sight. You can test the charge by listening for the buzzer when you push the appropriate button, or by using a test light.

When the time has come to train the dog, or more often, re-train the dog, place the real collar around the dog's neck and wait awhile before proceeding. Position yourself where you can see the dog without the dog knowing you are watching. From then on you simply need to wait for the improper behavior. When it occurs, sound the buzzer. If the behavior continues, hit the shocker. Expect a yelp the first couple of times. The dog will be genuinely surprised and confused. However, after as few as one or two shocks that are always given in association with a specific behavior (for example, crawling under a fence or chasing a lamb), the dog should simply avoid that behavior.

The main requirements for this method of training are patience and precise timing. You have to be prepared to correct a problem repeatedly and promptly and you must be present to catch the dog misbehaving. If the behavior you want to stop only occurs infrequently, you might set up an artificial situation to encourage it. For example, if the problem is that the dog chases sheep, put the dog in with some new sheep. They will tend to run away from him, encouraging him to chase them.

We must repeat that for all of the potential good that can be obtained from an electronic collar, there are possible hazards. If you are not consistent in the administration of the buzz and/or shock, the dog will not associate a specific behavior with the signals. Work on one behavioral problem at a time. Don't decide to cure a barking problem and an escaping problem at the same time or you will confuse the dog. Appropriate use of an electric collar can lead to prompt, and often permanent, correction of a nagging problem.

There are anti-barking collars on the market that are not operated by the owner, but are activated by a vibration sensor built into the collar. Most of these collars will allow a dog to bark a few times before emitting a warning beep, followed by a shock if the dog continues to bark. Some collars will spray citronella or another nasty smelling substance to interrupt the dog's barking sequence. These collars can be used whenever the owner wishes the dog to remain silent, and do not prevent the dog from barking when they are not wearing the collar. Critics of bark collars feel that dogs should not be punished when they need to bark for good reasons, such as warning off a predator or intruder—and they have a valid point. Most owners who use anti-bark collars live in urban areas that have noise restrictions, and the question arises about the validity of keeping working dogs, that bark in order to do their job, in such an environment. All livestock protection dogs are barkers—that is the nature of these breeds.

We concluded the Preface with a request for your assistance. Our contact information appears at the end of this book. If you learn of other creative solutions to problems, please let us know. Advancing the science and art of livestock protection dog management requires cooperation and sharing of ideas. We'll happily use future editions of this book to share your ideas and experiences with others.

Puppy Testing and Selection

CHAPTER 8

Most owners give little thought to the selection of an individual puppy. They may spend months pouring over material on different breeds in order to determine which best suits their needs. When confronted by a litter of adorable puppies most choices are made with the heart rather than the head. It's hard to resist the pup that comes bounding toward you, eyes sparkling and tail wagging. Perhaps the quiet one wins your heart, by cocking his head and looking at you with sad puppy eyes. Yet how can you be sure that this dog will suit your needs? Will he mature into the livestock guardian that you need? Will he develop into a loving and loyal home companion? Puppy selection can be the very first step in forming a bond between owner and dog. We have all seen owners with dogs that are perfectly suited to their lifestyle. For these fortunate people, dog ownership is a delight and a joy. However, breeders too often hear horror stories of a pup relegated to a solitary existence in a backyard pen because he just doesn't seem to fit in with the family. The pup's exuberant behavior, so appealing during those first few months, now drives his owners to distraction.

Many breeders have begun to use puppy aptitude tests (PAT) to provide themselves and their buyers more information about individual pups in their litters. They have found that, besides observing the behavior of pups, standardized testing provides another way to evaluate the future personality of each pup. At first we were skeptical about such tests. Like many breeders, we watched our litters closely and felt that we could already make good guesses about our puppies' personalities. After administering the tests, we discovered that they confirmed our own observations. More importantly, aptitude testing provided an organized, objective means of evaluating the puppies. After fifteen-plus years of experience with this type of testing, we are pleased with the results.

While aptitude testing has become more common in recent years, its use has been largely confined to determining companion qualities. How, we wondered, could the test be used to determine which puppies would become successful protectors of livestock? What characteristics should we expect to see in a pup best suited for this use? Since such research had never been undertaken before, we set out to learn as much as possible about the qualities inherent in a successful livestock guardian. We experimented with a variety of tests. We kept records of our tests and tracked the progress of our puppies. In addition, we formulated a test in which we exposed our puppies to livestock and noted their reactions. We feel now that we can more accurately predict which of our puppies to place in working homes and which would benefit more from a companion home environment.

We have come to believe that aptitude testing is a reliable and valuable tool for both breeders and owners. The investment of ten to twenty minutes per puppy after setup seems a small price to pay for the advantage of matching puppies with the right owners. There's an added incentive for breeders, too. There are buyers who request a "pick of the litter" pup and are willing to pay a little extra. With puppy aptitude testing, there can be more than one "pick" pup. Potentially, there will be a pick of litter male and female for livestock protection work, as well as pick male and female for domestic companions. This is an all-win situation for the breeder, the buyers and the dogs. We recommend that new owners purchase from a breeder who takes the time to test her puppies. If you are interested in buying a pup from a litter that has not been evaluated, you may wish to ask for permission to conduct the test yourself.

WHAT IS APTITUDE TESTING?

In aptitude testing, puppies are put through a series of exercises where their reactions are noted and evaluated. In theory, a puppy at about seven weeks of age will behave in a manner that predicts his adult personality. Scores will depend to some extent on how the pups have been socialized and stimulated during the weeks prior to the test, and there can be differences between breeds and lines within breeds. In general, though, aptitude tests provide a fairly good indication of a pup's reactions to people and mild stress. They are also reasonably accurate in determining the submissive and aggressive tendencies of puppies. As such, they can help us determine which home would be best suited to the pup and what type of training would be most effective. We must remember, however, that it's impossible to predict the environmental factors that each pup may face once he goes to his new home. For this reason, we must bear in mind that aptitude testing is only a useful indicator, not a foolproof predictor. It is up to the breeder to match the most suitable puppy to each owner. The breeder should also explain the PAT results so that the new owner can use appropriate methods to train and handle their puppy.

The basic test that we and most other professionals use was originally published by William E. Campbell. In his book, Behavior Problems in Dogs, Mr. Campbell presents a test designed to aid in puppy selection. In addition, we also use a test designed by Jack and Wendy Volhard to determine obedience aptitude. The result is the Puppy Aptitude Test (PAT) described by Melissa Bartlett in Pure-Bred Dogs - American Kennel Gazette. In our continuing attempt to learn more about this fascinating subject, we have also added the "barrier" test, devised by trainer Gail Tamases Fisher. This test is an attempt to determine inherent intelligence or problem-solving ability.

We have developed a test for evaluating the reaction of protection breed puppies to livestock. While we can give you our observations after administering this test, it is not as easy to score as the more standardized tests. This is primarily because of the different behaviors that the livestock might show. Still, it may provide important clues of future interaction with livestock and aid breeders whose goal is to produce a consistent line of reliable livestock guardians.

HOW TO CONDUCT THE PUPPY APTITUDE TEST

You will need one person to administer the test and one to score results. Ideally the tester should be a stranger to the puppies. Select a location that's new to the puppies and as free from distractions as possible. Some old carpeting would provide good footing for the pups, or you can perform the tests outside if the weather permits. If your pups have been raised at the barn, testing them on a slippery tile floor in your house may be too distracting and stressful. A different place in the barn or somewhere outside yet near to where they have been kept perhaps would be a better choice. You want to provide mild stress, not a traumatic experience. You will also need to gather together a small, soft ball, a spoon, a metal pan, an umbrella, a small towel or an old sock stuffed with rags tied to a string and the score sheets provided in this chapter. Have the tester familiarize herself with the score sheets so she will have an idea of what reactions to look for.

Pups are typically around seven weeks when they are tested. The tester takes one pup at a time to the test area, speaking reassuringly and handling the pup gently to establish a friendly atmosphere. Urine spots or stools produced during the test should be ignored until the puppy has left the area. Direct eye contact should also be avoided, except during the dominance or restraint exercises. Even then, eye contact should not be turned into a staring contest, which the pup may interpret as a threat. The tester should try to make the entire procedure fun for the puppies. Each puppy should be treated equally. If a puppy is particularly upset or frightened, the tester might want to take a little more time at the beginning to let the pup get used to her.

There are five parts to each of the general aptitude and the obedience aptitude portions of the test. We will describe the basic procedure for administering each part, and then explain how to interpret PAT scores.

General Aptitude Test

1. Social Attraction

As soon as the test area has been entered, place the puppy in the center. Back up four to six feet in the direction of the door or gate. Crouch down facing the puppy and call him, encouraging him by gently clapping your hands and talking to him. This should attract the puppy to you. Note how quickly the pup comes, whether his tail is up or down, or if he fails to come to you, or only comes after exploring. These observations should be noted on the score sheet.

2. Following

Place the puppy beside you. Walk away from him slowly, taking short steps, watching closely to see if he follows. Be certain that the pup sees you walk away. You may return to the pup and walk away several times to gauge his reaction, and encourage him verbally if you wish. Make sure you treat each puppy the same way.

3. Restraint Dominance

Crouch down beside the pup and roll him onto his back. Place one or both hands gently over his chest. You want to hold the pup in this restrained position for thirty seconds, or until any initial resistance has abated and he has turned his head away from you. Note if the pup struggles or accepts this position.

PAT – Following test. Photo by David Sims.

PAT – Restraint dominance test. Photo by David Sims.

4. Social Dominance

Crouch down beside the pup and position him so that he sits facing you at a forty-five degree angle. Place your head close to him and stroke gently, starting at the head and moving to the back. Continue stroking until the pup has established a recognizable behavior before you score. Stroke for a full thirty seconds, whether or not the puppy moves away. You may speak to him, but be sure to do the same for each pup. Some pups will leave and then return.

5. Elevation Dominance

Cradle the pup. Your interlaced fingers should support his chest and belly. Elevate him just off the ground for 30 seconds, pointing his head away from you. The pup's response to this total lack of control is noted.

Obedience Aptitude Test

The second part of the PAT is the obedience aptitude portion of the test. This also consists of five parts.

PAT – Elevation dominance test. Photo by David Sims.

1. Retrieving

Kneel beside the pup and attract his attention with a small, soft ball. When the pup is watching, toss the ball four to six feet, on a diagonal, away from and in front of him. Score the response. If the pup does not respond, repeat the exercise twice more. When the pup goes for the ball, step back two feet and encourage him to come to you.

2. Touch Sensitivity

Take one of the pup's front feet and spread two toes to expose the webbing. With your finger and thumb, press the webbing until you get a response. Begin lightly and increase the pressure, while you count slowly to ten or more. Stop as soon as the puppy pulls away or shows discomfort.

3. Sound Sensitivity

Leave the puppy and walk a few feet away. You want to make a sharp, loud noise to gauge the puppy's reaction. Striking a spoon once or twice on a metal pan usually works well. You may repeat this exercise a couple of times to make sure of the response. This test can also be used to verify if a pup may have physical hearing problems.

4. Chase Instinct (Sight Sensitivity)

Place the pup in the center of the room. Tie a string around a small towel or stuffed sock and drag it across the floor, a few feet from the puppy. If the puppy grabs the sock with his mouth, stop pulling. Score the response.

5. Stability

Place the pup in the center of the area. Hold a closed umbrella four feet from the pup and point it at him. Open the umbrella smoothly and quickly and set it down. A spring-operated, self-opening umbrella is too fast and sudden for this purpose. Allow the pup to investigate. Don't be surprised if the puppy becomes startled when the umbrella is first opened. Score the response after the umbrella is set down.

SCORING THE PUPPY APTITUDE TEST

You may find a wide variation in the aptitudes and personalities of the puppies you tested. Breeders are often amazed at the differences found within a single litter. In glancing over each pup's score sheet, you will most

SAMPLE PUPPY APTITUDE TEST SCORE CARD

TEST AND RESPONSE	Score	Puppy ID
Social Attraction		
Comes readily, tail/ears/body posture up, may jump up	1	
Comes readily, tail/ears up, licks hands	2	
Comes readily, tail up, may wiggle upon reaching tester	3	
Comes readily, tail down, ears may be back, may wiggle	4	
Comes hesitant, tail/ears down	5	
Comes after much encouragement	6	
Does not come at all, or goes away	7	
Explores first before coming to tester (YES/NO)		
If Yes, for how long, where in relation to tester		
Following		
Follows readily, tail/ears/body posture up, gets underfoot	1	
Follows readily, tail/ears up, tries to keep up	2	
Follows readily, tail down, ears may be back, may stay behind	3	
Follows hesitant, tail/ears down, may stop and start again	4	
Follows after much encouragement	5	
Does not follow or goes away	6	
Restraint Dominance		
Struggles fiercely, flails, tries to bite	1	
Struggles fiercely, flails, may settle briefly, may make eye contact	2	
Struggles/settles, may be vocal, makes some eye contact	3	
Some struggle, beginning or end, heart rate steady or up a little	4	
No struggle, heart rate steady or up a little	5	
No struggle, strains to avoid eye contact, heart rate usually up	6	
Social Dominance		
Jumps, growls, may try to bite, may be vocal, posture up	1	
Jumps, may paw, may nip and lick, tail/ears often up	2	
Cuddles up to tester, nuzzles, tail may wag, ears may be back	3	
Wiggles around tester, may lick hands	4	
Appears hesitant, ears/tail down, may roll over	5	
Freezes in place or leaves tester, avoidance	6	
Elevation Dominance		
Struggles fiercely, attempts to bite, growls	1	
Struggles fiercely, may vocalize	2	
Hangs relaxed, no struggle, calm, heartbeat steady	3	
Settled but some struggle (beginning or end), heartbeat elevated	4	
Slight struggle, heartbeat elevated, head/eye may be still	5	
No struggle, limbs frozen, heartbeat elevated	6	

SAMPLE PUPPY APTITUDE TEST SCORE CARD

TEST AND RESPONSE	Score	Puppy ID
Retrieving		
Chases ball, picks it up, runs away, posture up, may pounce	1	
Chases ball, stands over it, doesn't return	2	
Chases ball, returns with it to tester, no prompting (to or near)	3	
Chases ball, may pick it up, returns to tester without ball	4	
Starts to chase ball, loses interest	5	
Does not chase ball, may actively avoid watching ball	6	
Touch Sensitivity		
8-10 counts before response	1	
6-7 counts before response	2	
5-6 counts before response	3	
2-4 counts before response	4	
1-2 counts before response	5	
Sound Sensitivity		
Listens, locates sound, walks toward it barking/growling	1	
Listens, locates sound, barks, posture up	2	
Listens, locates sound, shows curiosity, walks toward it	3	
Listens, locates sound, ears up	4	
Startles, backs away, ears/tail down, may try to hide	5	
Ignores sound, shows no response/curiosity	6	
Chase Instinct (Sight Sensitivity)		
Looks, attacks, bites, may growl, shakes rag after it stops	1	
Looks, tail/ears up, follows, may bark, bite at rag	2	
Looks curiously, attempts to investigate, tail up, may bite	3	
Looks, may follow, hesitant, tail/ears down, may growl	4	
Tail tucked, backs away, tries to hide	5	
Runs away, actively avoids rag	6	
Stability		
Walks forward, tail up, attacks, may growl/bark, posture up	1	
Walks forward, tail up, mouths	2	
Walks forward, attempts to investigate	3	
Looks curiously, stays put	4	
Goes away, tail down, hides	5	
Ignores, shows no curiosity	6	
Energy Level		
High—Continually runs, pounces, wiggles, paws	1	
Medium—Mostly trots, occasionally runs, pounces	2	
Low—Walks slowly, sits quietly, remains in position	3	
Stress—Stands rigidly, eyes roll, tail down, ears back	4	

SAMPLE PUPPY APTITUDE TEST SCORE CARD

TEST AND RESPONSE		Score	Puppy ID

Barrier Test (Problem solving)

Responses (No scoring)	Finds exit, but does not go through
Anxious, tries to go through screen	Finds exit, goes through immediately
Anxious, paces back and forth	Calm, does not try to leave
Anxious, whimpers, yelps	Calm, looks for exit quietly
Anxious, does not move	Length of time to find exit and leave (seconds)

RESPONSE TO LIVESTOCK

Passive Stock, No Eye Contact with Puppy

	Score
Curious, tail up, makes eye contact, goes to stock, barks, jumps or bites at stock	1
Curious, tail up, makes eye contact, goes to stock	2
Curious, tail up, makes eye contact	3
Fearful or cautious, looks at stock then away, tail down	4
Leaves, stays away, watches stock from a distance	5
Ignores stock	6

Active Stock, Eye Contact with Puppy

	Score
Curious, tail up, makes eye contact, goes to stock, barks, jumps or bites at stock	1
Curious, tail up, makes eye contact, goes to stock	2
Curious, tail up, makes eye contact	3
Fearful or cautious, looks at stock then away, tail down	4
Leaves, stays away, watches stock from a distance	5
Ignores stock	6

Aggressive Stock, Eye Contact, Stomping, Lowered Head

	Score
Curious, tail up, makes eye contact, goes to stock, barks, jumps or bites at stock	1
Curious, tail up, makes eye contact, goes to stock	2
Curious, tail up, makes eye contact	3
Fearful or cautious, looks at stock then away, tail down	4
Leaves, stays away, watches stock from a distance	5
Ignores stock	6

Aggressive Stock, Charges Puppy

	Score
Stands ground, growls or barks, keeps eye contact	1
Stands then moves out of way, growls or barks	2
Moves out of way, tail up, not worried	3
Moves out of way, tail down, avoids eye contact	4
Moves out of way, tail down, lies down or rolls over, avoids eye contact	5
Runs and hides	6

PAT - Stability test. Photo by David Sims.

likely see a strong pattern. If there is no clear pattern, it may indicate that the pup wasn't feeling well and should be retested in a couple of days. If a pattern still doesn't emerge, it simply means that the test scores are difficult to interpret, or possibly that the pup will be somewhat unpredictable in behavior.

Age at the time of testing can influence the pups' scores. Ideally, the litter should be tested when they are between seven and eight weeks old. As the pups grow, they usually become more confident, and this can change the PAT scores. The same may hold true for pups who are retested. When retesting is necessary, do not test more than twice a week.

Remember, the scoring system does not use a pass or fail approach, so adding up the numbers is meaningless. No dog fails the test or does better than his littermates. Instead, the scoring system simply indicates ranges of behavior. This information can be used by the breeder to place a pup in the best environment for his particular temperament, and by owners to tailor their handling and training approaches. Here is how to interpret your scores, in the context of a companion dog:

Mostly 1's
This dog is extremely dominant and exhibits aggressive tendencies. He may be quick to bite and would not be suitable in a home with children or the elderly. If the dog also scored one or two in the touch sensitivity

exercise, he may be difficult to train. This is not the pup for an inexperienced handler. His new owner should be a competent trainer who is fully prepared to establish himself as a leader.

Mostly 2's

This dog is dominant and may be provoked to bite. He should respond well to firm, consistent and fair handling and is best suited to a household composed of adults. Once he learns to respect his master, this dog is likely to be a loyal pet. Dogs in this category are often bouncy and outgoing. They may, however, prove too active for the elderly and too dominant for homes with small children.

Mostly 3's

This dog easily accepts humans as leaders. He adapts well to new situations and is generally good with children and the elderly, although he may be inclined to be active. A dog that falls in this category is the best prospect for an average owner, who will appreciate his commonsense approach to life. He should also be a good obedience prospect (within the parameters of the breed).

Mostly 4's

This dog is submissive and will generally adapt to most households. He may be slightly less outgoing than the dog who scored mostly 3's. In general, this dog makes a good companion for children and should respond well to training.

Mostly 5's

This dog is extremely submissive. He will need special handling to help build his confidence and bring him out of his shell. Dogs of this type do not respond well to change and confusion, and are best suited to a routine, structured environment. The dog is usually safe around children and will probably bite only when severely stressed. This type of dog is not a good choice for the beginner, since he frightens more easily. The owner must be patient when introducing the dog to new experiences.

Mostly 6's and 7's

Dogs in these categories can be shy, aloof and highly independent. They generally are not affectionate. In fact, they may even dislike petting and cuddling. In a companion situation, it's more difficult to establish a relationship with one of these dogs. Avoid placing this pup in a home with children who are prone to forcing attention on the dog. This is not a dog for the beginner. He may be best suited for a place with a lot of space and little human traffic.

THE PUPPY APTITUDE TEST
AND THE LIVESTOCK GUARDIAN

How do livestock protection dogs generally score on the PAT? While our own experience has been primarily with Akbash Dogs, we believe that our observations will assist owners of other livestock protection breeds. In our studies, we have found very few dogs that show highly social/dominant traits, that is, scoring mostly 1's and 2's. In general, we have found that livestock protection dogs tend to be more independent in nature. Most pups tested fall in the 3-5 range, and 6's and 7's are not uncommon.

How do you determine which puppy to send to the 6,000-acre ranch in Texas and which to the 20-acre sheep farm in Ontario? We have found that the quieter, less active and more reserved pups are best suited to the task of protecting livestock, especially on small holdings. Those dogs who show less tendency to want human interaction are also well suited to ranch life. In addition, we look for the independent dog, which will require less direction from people. In this situation, the dog that seems less oriented toward people may be more likely to stay with the livestock, rather than seeking human companionship. The pups scoring 6's and 7's would also do best in situations that provide the most stability and routine, and wide-open spaces. These pups appear to be more easily stressed and less adaptable. On the other hand, high-energy pups may also have a place on ranches or areas of open grazing where predators abound. These dogs will have to use a great deal of energy patrolling huge tracts of land, so their higher activity levels can be put to good use if they are not overly socially attracted to people.

Which dogs are best suited to a life in suburbia? The more active, bouncy and outgoing pups are apt to perform best in a domestic setting. For the family companion, we look for those pups who are particularly fond of people. Be sure, however, to consider the temperament of the owners, as well as the pup. Ask about their family lifestyle. Some owners would be more comfortable with a quiet, laid-back pup than a more active individual, so pups scoring 3's and 4's would be most suitable.

In examining the PAT scores, you will inevitably find some pups that score in between the ideal companion and livestock guardian. You may well find several pups within a litter that can successfully be placed in either a farm or home situation. Ultimately, there is no substitute for the observations you have made over the past few weeks. The test scores should confirm your feelings about the pups. The amount of early handling, stimulation and socialization can also affect the scores, so be aware if any pups received more attention than others as it will likely be reflected in the test results.

THE BARRIER TEST

The barrier test is essentially an exercise in problem solving. In this test, the pup is placed behind a barrier that has an opening off to one side or behind him. The pup should be able to see through the barrier. We use a hinged wire screen that meets the wall at one end, but leaves a space between the wall and screen at the other end. The pup is placed in the center, behind the screen. The tester remains in front of the screen and encourages the pup to come out. The pup can be motivated by whatever means is appropriate. Calling the pup is sufficient for some, while others need to be enticed with food. To get to the tester, the pup must find the exit, and this requires

Village shepherd and breeder, Zafer Cicek with his winning Kangal puppy at the annual Kangal Festival. Photo by Sue Kocher.

him to turn his back and walk away before he can approach the person. Note the pup's reactions to the exercise and the time it takes him to find the exit.

While this test should give an overall indication of a puppy's intelligence, it is not as easy to score as the PAT. Clearly, a bright, motivated puppy will figure his way around the barrier quickly. We have, however, noted a variation in the degree of individual motivation. Some seem intent on joining the tester, while others are content to stay behind the barrier. This is particularly true with those pups that are less people-oriented. We also discovered a problem using the same location for each pup tested. Some pups may have used their noses to trace the route taken by the previous pups. The solution is to move the barrier to different test sites within the room and damp-mop the floor to minimize scents.

THE LIVESTOCK TEST

Small flock owners may have some difficulty administering and scoring this test due to the variable reactions of their livestock. For the livestock test you should use a young lamb, goat kid or chicken that is known to remain calm in the presence of dogs. Using young or small stock ensures that the pups will not be hurt or frightened by an aggressive, charging animal. We have included score sheets for four different behaviors that livestock might display: 1) passive stock, which make no eye contact with the puppy; 2) active stock, which make eye contact with the puppy, but do not approach; 3) aggressive stock, which not only make eye contact with the puppy, but also stomp and lower their heads; and 4) very aggressive stock, which make eye contact and charge. If aggression should occur, be prepared to protect the puppy and terminate this aspect of the test at once.

As you can see from the score sheets, responses vary from 1 to 6. Ideally, this test should be a good indicator of which pups are most apt to be aggressive toward livestock, even if the aggression is based on defensive reactions. These pups may be poor candidates for work with stock. Also in question are those pups who totally ignore the stock. Before discounting such a pup, however, you may wish to retest. Possibly the puppy was feeling poorly for the first test, he may have been distracted by more interesting things around him or he was frozen with fear. Pups that seem unusually fearful may have already had a bad experience and should be observed carefully. Perhaps you can discover the cause of the fear. If an entire litter scores predominately in the 1's and 2's, be wary of selecting any of these pups for livestock work.

KEEP TESTING IN PERSPECTIVE

As valuable as puppy testing may be, remember that it is only a tool in evaluating a litter. You should still try to see the sire and dam, if at all possible. Ask about the temperaments of both parents. If you want a live-stock protection dog, your best bet is to select a puppy from two working parents. By combining the advice given in Chapter Three with these apti-tude testing methods, you will have improved your chances of getting the dog you want.

A Great Pyrenees breeder we've talked with includes another test. Puppies are placed on a foreign surface to determine their self-confidence. Confident puppies may be curious about a strange surface, but won't cringe in fear or become paralyzed when placed on it. Chicken wire fencing or a sheet of plastic can be used. Others may employ the same tests as we have described, but want more outgoing, confident, and yes, even aggressive, dogs for livestock protection. They use the same test, then select pups with lower scores (1's, 2's and 3's). It is possible however, that pups of one breed who score 1's and 2's may mature into what the 3's of another breed become.

As we collect more data in the future, we may find breed and even sex differences in how pups score. However, it is extremely difficult to compare results when tests are not uniformly administered, when pups have such variable early environments, and perhaps most important, when mature dogs have had such vastly different life experiences. Academicians interest-ed in canine behavior have studied PAT for a variety of companion dog breeds. Preliminary reports (conference proceedings, research abstracts) suggest that there is little or no correlation between a PAT score and adult personalities. We have little experience with puppy aptitude testing of breeds such as terriers, retrievers and hounds so we cannot comment on their findings. Also, we have not performed a rigorous, blind comparison of our own PAT scores with adult personalities of the dogs we have tested. We'd love to do this but the expense would be considerable. We continue to promote PAT, however, because for us it works.

We may never be able to tease out the strictly genetic factors con-tributing to adult behavior. The best any breeder can do is to start with good working stock, select the best possible pup for each situation, and provide good training advice and support to their buyers. After that, responsibility shifts to each owner to guide and mold his pup into the best possible dog he can be.

The Family Companion

Most people who are attracted to livestock protection dogs as companions are looking for an unusual breed that offers protection and loyalty. They are often disillusioned with the health and temperament problems of more conventional guard dogs like German Shepherd Dogs, Rottweilers and Doberman Pinschers—breeds that in recent years have come under more public scrutiny due to aggressive and sometimes fatal attacks on people, and on children in particular. There can be a perception that livestock protection dogs are more gentle and not as aggressive. Some people are taken with the beauty of livestock protection dogs; others simply like the idea of a large-sized rare breed. Although as many as thirty percent of our pups become companion dogs, they were not bred for that purpose. Many livestock protection dogs have a very independent nature, which is necessary for guarding livestock, and this may translate into indifference or stubbornness in the pet dog. Others have proven too dominant and aggressive for the average home. Soft-natured people and children are often unable to control this type of dog. There is no question most livestock protection breeds do not make easy or ideal companion dogs for the average owner. However, for those who are prepared to research the right breed and select just the right pup and who have the situation to suit such a dog and the experience and attitude to handle one, the advantages offered by a livestock protection dog can justify taking the extra care and time to raise one of these pups.

THE MYTH OF DUAL PURPOSE BREEDS

Most of the letters and phone calls we receive from pet owners reflect happiness and the secure feeling that comes with having a livestock protection dog companion. However, enough of these dogs raised as pets have created problems that we shall make frequent references within this chapter to your need for control over the dog at all times, beginning with the young puppy. There are far too many livestock protection dogs ending up in rescue situations because their owners did not research the breed adequately and/or could not control them. Some breed associations do not recommend that protection dogs be used as pets while others promote their breed as ideal for ranch, farm, home and show ring. The fact is, over time a number of breeds will have lines which will excel either at guarding livestock or at being companions and suitable for the show ring. Great Pyrenees, as an example, have been used for many years both as family pets and for livestock protection. However, it has been reported that a number of the dogs coming from companion and show lines have failed to protect livestock from dog attacks. Breeding for mild-mannered, sociable companion dogs is usually at cross purposes from breeding for dogs that will have the self-confidence and aggressive drive to actively repel formidable predators such as wolves and bears. We know there are excellent working Great Pyrenees that are bred for guarding livestock, and that dogs from the same lines can become decent companions. However, the reverse often is not true. And this applies to all of the breeds—we are now seeing softer, companion lines being developed within some of the tougher Turkish breeds as well. Such dogs with less aggressive drive may fit another niche of working dogs—small holdings where the dog has very little room to work and there is a lot of human traffic. This would include small farms of one to twenty acres at the edge of town, with small pens and pastures. In this case, a dog with lots of energy and drive would likely become so frustrated, he would engage in destructive behavior. A milder temperament would be more appropriate.

It is our opinion that "dual purpose" breeds, that is, those where the association promotes both working and show attributes, inevitably end up with greater emphasis on the show dog, at the expense of working ability and good health. For one thing, there is a far greater market demand for companion and show dogs than there is for legitimate working dogs. Since judging dogs in a show setting rarely provides any testing for temperament or health status, and in fact, penalizes dogs that are overly aggressive, the emphasis is on the conformation of the dog. On that basis, dogs that may be riddled with genetic defects and poor temperament can become champions of their breed. While we down play the value of show champions, we believe breeders should use a standard to breed to and emphasize the soundness and temperament of their breeding stock. Show venues can be useful for the socialization of young dogs and education of the public about the various breeds. Some national kennel clubs, such as the United Kennel Club of the United States (U.K.C.), make provisions for working breeds, emphasizing with their educational efforts the importance of good temperament. However, it is impossible to discern the correct working qualities of a livestock protection breed based on performance in a show ring. Unlike the herding trials for breeds like the Border Collie, there are no controlled tests devised that can determine the abilities of a livestock guardian. Only observing a dog at work in the field, in real-life conditions, faced by real threats, will tell us if that dog is truly a champion of his flock.

Even with the warnings that many of these dogs are not suitable as companions in an urban setting, we must admit that the protection breeds can adapt well to domestic life because of their calm nature and their flexibility in bonding to and protecting people as well as livestock. There seem to be a few less sociable strains within the livestock protection breeds found in North America. For example, some Akbash Dogs, Komondorok and Maremmas have been identified as excessively shy or dominant. Extremes in personality are probably a result of not selecting against those traits in the original lines of Asian and European breeding stock. Breeders in North America want to have a predictable, reliable product to offer, so they are working to recognize and eliminate overly aggressive or shy lines of dogs. Breeds like the Great Pyrenees and Kuvasz that, in many cases, have not been used to guard livestock for many generations and have been selected for their sociability with people and other dogs, may have a higher percentage of individuals more suited as companion dogs. Be aware that there are individuals in all these breeds that display extremes in behavior, which is why you should learn as much as possible about the behavioral pedigree of any pup you are considering, and only buy from knowledgeable breeders. There are breeders who specialize in providing dogs to companion homes. For the greatest chance at success, make sure the parents have a suitable temperament for the companion home, and ask for references of other people who have already purchased their dogs for that purpose.

THE IDEAL COMPANION HOME

What is the ideal companion home for a livestock protection dog? First we'll begin by describing what it is not. It is not an apartment, no matter where the apartment is located. It is not a small home with a small yard or no yard. It is not a home without a fenced yard. The ideal home will have a very large yard or acreage, surrounded by a secure, high fence—five feet or higher would be best. Owners should be prepared to deal with barking. These are guard dogs—guard dogs often bark while doing their job. If neighbors live too close, owners should be prepared to keep their dog indoors, especially at night, if they end up with a noisy dog. Ideally, they will have enough land around them that barking will not disturb any neighbors, and frequent animal and human traffic will not disturb and frustrate their dog. Owners should have previous experience with large, strong-willed, guard-type breeds, and no one in the family should be afraid of large dogs. They should be prepared to spend a great deal of time training and socializing the puppy, which means having lots of people over to visit, and taking the pup out frequently to various locations to meet with a variety of other people and dogs. Owners should be prepared for displays of aggression towards threatening people and animals. If the idea that the dog might kill a squirrel or rabbit or even a stray cat is abhorrent to an owner, it is best to stay away from these breeds. They can be trained to leave other animals alone, but if the owner isn't skilled or patient enough to do so, they could have a few unpleasant surprises in store for them.

The rest of the chapter will be devoted to raising a livestock protection dog as a companion; however, we strongly encourage all new owners to use the bibliography at the end of the book to find and use other resources on training and behavior.

PREPARATIONS: START WITH A GOOD FENCE

As with any large breed, owners will want to have a good fence around their property. This means a fence tall enough that the dog cannot jump or climb out (five-plus feet), with no gaps at ground level or openings larger than six to eight inches through which a pup could squeeze. In rural areas, a fence can be reinforced with inside strands of electric wiring; in urban areas, radio fences can be used for reinforcement. A good fence will sharply define the territory for the dog, as well as prevent undesired interactions with people or other animals. A sign on the gate indicating the presence of a large protection dog would be a neighborly gesture. Allowing the dog to roam is dangerous and, in most cases, lethal for the dog.

We do not approve of chaining any breed of dog in the backyard. However, this method of confinement would be far more likely to prove disastrous with a protection breed of dog. A chained dog becomes frustrated without a reasonable territory and people to bond with. In Hungarian Dog Breeds, authors Sarkany and Ocsag warn that chained Kuvaszok are likely to become uncontrollable. Far better to allow the dog to fully integrate with the family. For a guardian dog, a well-fenced yard is a must.

Two dog doors allow access to back porch and fenced backyard. Dogs can be blocked into the porch in or out of the backyard and house. In this photo, the closer dog door has its plexiglass barrier in place, while the farther door is open for business. A flexible plastic cover is held in place by magnets, and the dogs easily push the cover aside to walk through. Dog doors provide an opportunity for dogs to be so much happier. They can guard property and family more effectively when they can come and go from the house, and of course, dogs can relieve themselves without human intervention. In this photo, the porch is unheated, so there is minimal heat loss during the winter as a result of having dog doors. Photo by David Sims.

SETTING THE RIGHT TONE

Assuming that your pup is intended as a companion, and perhaps for obedience competition, is there anything special about how he should be handled and trained as a young dog? Yes! The pup must realize that you are in charge. Be loving and kind but always remain firm and consistent. You control all resources for the pup (food, shelter, attention) and he must always acknowledge this by respecting you. These pups are most comfortable with rules and will gladly follow them when you insist.

There are also a couple of expectations you shouldn't have. Retrievers they are not. Whether you have fun or competition in mind, most protection dogs do not show an aptitude for retrieving. Of course, there are exceptions, but don't expect this ability. Second, protection dogs are often diggers. They dig to scratch out a cool place to lie on a hot day, or because they are bored and are trying to escape. So be forewarned. Bored protection dogs have been known to excavate craters.

To set the stage for a successful relationship with a protection dog, the family should agree in advance what the pup will be allowed to do, and where and when. Meet as a family to plan your canine strategies. Design a daily routine and decide who will be in charge of what. The puppy should have a place of refuge, perhaps a bed in a corner of the house, or a doghouse outside. Meals should be regular, and the pup allowed frequent opportunities to relieve himself if he is kept indoors. If you are going to limit where the dog can go when inside the house, choose obvious boundaries. For example, many owners allow their dog wherever there is tile or linoleum flooring, but not carpet or wood. Once you have chosen the boundaries, make certain that all members of the family enforce them. Child-proof gates across doorways can be useful when training the pup to remain in certain areas.

ESTABLISHING THE HIERARCHY

An outgoing, self-confident puppy that has been selected as a companion dog, and perhaps with obedience or agility competition in mind, may also have a dominant personality. If this type of pup is not handled properly as a youngster, he could end up showing dominance aggression towards people and other animals he perceives as weaker than himself. Whether or not your pup has this personality trait, never allow him to win any confrontations or refuse your commands. The question comes down to who is in control. Control is partly accomplished by anticipating your pup's reactions and making sure he is not in a position to disobey you. For instance, when you are first formally training your pup to come, have him in a small enclosed area, or on a lead, so you can easily reach him if he doesn't come to you. Once a pup has learned he can ignore your wishes, he will exercise his "selective hearing" whenever he thinks he can get away with it or when he is more interested in whatever he is already doing. Livestock protection dogs are intelligent and they will learn your weaknesses, even as pups. The more dominant ones can eventually turn the tables and become top-ranking members in their families, human or animal. Remember, the naughty little 15-pound pup may someday weigh 120 pounds and have a strong bite.

There is an old adage that "nothing in life is free." If you exercise this saying, so that your dog has to do something to "earn" his meals, entrance or exit from the house, or anything else you do for him, you'll have a dog that respects you and is less likely to give you trouble. Let's illustrate with a specific example. A visitor staying with us for ten days was very taken by our four-year-old male Akbash Dog, Civa. Whenever he saw Civa, he broke into a "Good dog, good doggy!" and petted him profusely. Our visitor walked Civa each morning, and then put him back in his yard, while we were at work. On the fifth day of the visit, he reported that Civa had cocked his leg and urinated on his pants. Later, Civa growled at him when he tried to put him back in his yard. We asked our friend to change his tone with Civa, to be more assertive, and to only praise him after he had obeyed a command, such as having him sit before he was petted or allowed out the door. These simple changes worked. The visitor had no further problems with the dog.

Civa did not respect this person who was willing to give all sorts of rewards for no work. The same is true of inconsistent owners, as well as those who are "permissive" and "soft." Having the respect of the livestock guardian dog that shares your domicile is essential. These dogs only respect alpha figures, that is, leader-type personalities who are more dominant than they are. Leadership, and hence control, are established when your pet is a pup, and must be maintained throughout the dog's lifetime. A very dominant dog that is well controlled may still challenge your authority periodically, although not very seriously if you have established a strong leadership role. In this way, these dogs follow the instinctive rules of their predecessors, the wolves.

A final note on dominance. When applied to our relationship with dogs, this word does not imply cruelty or fighting. Achieving control over

A Polish Tatra on vacation with the family. Photo by Carol A. Wood.

a dog should never involve anger or aggression on the part of the owner. An owner who is in control and has the respect of his dog has the obligation to show kindness, care and love to this dog. In a family pack, the dog is a member that relies on his human leaders to provide him with the necessities of life. A harmonious pack will also accord respect to the dog in return for his respect, his service and his willingness to accept his lower position in the hierarchy. Precisely how a dog is to be shown respect is yet another excellent topic for family discussion.

LEADERSHIP EXERCISES

As discussed earlier, there are several exercises you can perform to establish and maintain your leadership position over a pup. One is to lift him slightly off the ground by holding him firmly under the chest and belly until he is relaxed, then letting him down gently. When he is too heavy to lift, lean over his back, put one arm over his shoulder and under his chest, the other arm under his chest and just lift his front legs off the ground. He should submit to this loss of control and trust that you will let him go and not hurt him. As a small pup you can also roll him over on his back and hold him, hand on chest, until he is not struggling and has looked away from you. This is not meant to be a fight—be gentle but firm, and don't stare hard at him. When your puppy is relaxed or has submitted, you can either release him or you can rub his belly so it becomes a pleasurable experience for him. If you continue to do this periodically as he matures, you will be able to do this to him as an adult.

Your pup should also be desensitized to physical handling. Open his mouth and have a look at his teeth, touch his teeth and tongue. Make sure

Trooper, an eight-month-old Kuvasz, accompanies a young friend at play time. Photo by Stuart Prisk.

to stroke his ears and lift them up so you are able to eventually put a cotton swab inside his ears for cleaning. Pick up each paw and gently squeeze his toes and the webbing between his toes, massage his legs, touch him all over so he gets used to this handling. You will want to be able to clip his toenails, so getting him used to having his feet handled is important. If he struggles, don't let him go. Insist on holding him until he has settled down. For pups who had received no or minimal handling earlier and begin to panic, you may want to have small treats on hand to distract them or reward them for complying. Clip one toenail at a time, if necessary, then treat and release. Males especially should tolerate being touched near their genitals. Gentle brushing, even if they don't need it, is also a good idea so the puppies get used to grooming early on.

One of the most important things to teach a pup is that you control his food. You can give it to him, you can take it away and you can expect him not to complain or attack you when you do so. This can be done by asking your pup to sit and wait while you put down his bowl of food and only allowing him to eat when you give him a release word like "okay." Seven-week-old pups can be taught this. You can also put your hand in the puppy's bowl while he is eating, and even feed him one piece of food at a time from his bowl. You should be able to pick up his bowl and put it back down without any growling.

The real test comes when you offer him a raw bone. Select a bone large enough that you can hold on to one end while he chews at the other. Take the bone away, then return it to him right away. If he growls, remove the bone and try again later. You can also work with two bones, offering him the second one while removing the first. This way he knows that you are just trading goodies and he will be less inclined to snap at the retreating bone and feel he is being cheated. Initially he doesn't know that you will return the bone to him. This is important since you never know when you will have to take a coveted article or treat away from him and not return it, such as that rotting fish he discovers on your beach walk. Unfortunately, many people get bitten by their own dogs over food. The canine instinct to protect food is strong and often overlooked; therefore, teaching your pup that he can trust you to give and take food from him any time is highly recommended.

With all these exercises, keep in mind that you should be able to do anything to your dog within reason and that he should learn to accept your handling. Never end any exercises with your dog struggling, or he will learn that he can make you stop what you are doing. As soon as the puppy submits for a few seconds, praise and release him. Now he has learned how to please you.

BASIC OBEDIENCE

Training your dog is more than just a good idea—it's essential. Things to consider include how much and what type of training is required to suit your needs. There are many good written texts and websites on training dogs, beginning with puppy training and working all the way to advanced obedience, agility, tracking and protection work. We will not attempt to present this material, but will point out a few traits that protection dogs possess that the pet owner should be aware of. An entire section of the Bibliography is devoted to training references. Participating in public obedience classes is preferable to training your dog on your own. In this instance, the training of a companion dog can be quite different from that of a livestock protection dog. You'll want your companion dog to be as socialized with other dogs as possible. In fact, early and continual socialization is essential if you want a dog you can take anywhere and know he will be under your control.

Pups can learn to sit on command as early as six weeks of age. By the time they are three months old, they can be taught to walk on a lead. This should be done gradually, first by putting some pressure on the collar while holding the pup, then following the pup around the house on a loose lead. Eventually, you can put some pressure on the leash and begin to guide the pup around. The pup may be frightened when he feels that first tug, so be patient and use lots of praise and encouragement and perhaps food treats as rewards. He will soon find that going with you is more pleasant than going in the opposite direction.

Use of the lead is essential when teaching the pup to come and to prevent chasing, both common problems with most breeds. In order to ensure that he will always come to you, begin teaching him the "come" command when your puppy first arrives. Each time you walk into a room or into his pen and see him, say, "Puppy, Come!" and reward him with praise and small food rewards when he obeys. You can also begin teaching the "sit" command by holding a treat over his head, slightly behind him, so he has to plant his butt down and look up. Once he is doing this reliably, you can add the word "sit" before giving him the treat. Eventually, you will not need to use treats, just praise. Practice the recall often; then release the pup to play or whatever he was doing, so he learns to associate something positive with coming to you. Never scold a pup that has just come to you when you called, no matter what horrible thing he just did. If you must punish the rascal for a misdeed, go to the pup. If you do this consistently you will be well on your way to teaching your pup to always come to you, no matter what he is doing.

Two other very useful commands that all companion dogs should know are "lie down" and "stay." Most dogs will enjoy obeying once they understand exactly what you want them to do. Teaching these exercises is accomplished as with any other breeds, so we refer you to the sources in the Bibliography. One difference between livestock protection dogs and some other breeds is that they are quickly bored by excessive repetition. Keep home training sessions short, say five to fifteen minutes at a time, and vary them to maintain the dog's interest. Tolerance to repeated exercises will vary between individuals. If you cannot retain their attention, change the exercise or quit for the time being. Some people use food rewards inter-mittently to keep their dogs motivated. Use food sparingly and do not reward the dog for each correct activity once he appears to have learned a command.

TRAINING EQUIPMENT

There is also the question of training equipment—types of collars, halters, leashes, harnesses. We firmly believe that choke chains should never be used to train a dog due to the damage they can inflict to the trachea and neck. Also, they are misused so frequently that many dogs develop resistance to them and even to training in general. Throw them out! Or use them to hang plants. Most training should be done with a flat collar that will neither slip off nor choke a dog. Pinch or prong collars may be used for older, particularly difficult dogs that for a variety of reasons cannot be controlled with a regular collar. Although pinch collars look far worse than choke collars, they do not damage the neck and are far more effective. They have been likened to power steering in a car. Head halters such as Promise, Halti and Gentle Leader can be used with certain dogs; however, they also have caused problems with wrenched necks and spines when used improperly or on the wrong dogs. Harnesses can be used for tracking work or pulling but are generally not useful for training regular commands. For more detailed information on training equipment, refer to

Suzanne Clothier's excellent web site, www.flyingdogpress.com or her published material (see Bibliography.)

HOUSE-TRAINING

Livestock protection breeds are fairly easy to house-train. We recommend that a new pup not have the run of the house, but be kept confined to a small area at first. A room with a linoleum or tile floor is best for this purpose. If a pup must be left alone for any length of time, he should be kept in a pen, indoors or out, or in a crate. If the area is small enough, the pup will tend not to soil his living space but will wait to be let out before relieving himself. Of course, he cannot wait forever, so you should be reasonable about the length of time you leave a young pup cooped up, especially during the day. To help him get through the night, withdraw water by around 8:00 P.M. (assuming that temperature and humidity are appropriate to do this). Also, if the conditions where the pup spent his first seven weeks or so of life were filthy, or if there wasn't a separate area to soil, he may not have a strong sense of cleanliness. If you must be gone long periods of time, providing a safely enclosed outdoor pen or kennel is advised.

Most pups will want to go outside to defecate and urinate. By watching the puppy you will be able to anticipate his needs and provide the opportunity for him to get outside at the right time. Puppies learn quickly once such a routine is established. Punishment for accidents is far less likely to be effective than praise for proper behavior and providing the opportunity to establish a routine. For more detailed tips on house-training, including the use of a crate, refer to the Bibliography.

CHEWING

Puppies often experience discomfort when they are losing their milk teeth at around four months of age. They will naturally want to chew on something to massage their gums. Knowing that this will happen, the wisest thing to do is provide safe, chewable objects for the pup, whether he is with you in the house or in a pen or crate. There are a number of dog toys available in pet stores, supermarkets, department stores and mail-order supply firms. These toys are made from cotton, latex rubber, hard nylon, rawhide and bone. We do not recommend cheap toys with squeakers built in unless you are present to supervise play periods. Puppies may become fascinated with the source of the squeak which they can remove from the toy and possibly swallow or—worse yet—inhale. Old socks stuffed with rags can also make a suitable, inexpensive toy. If you choose to stuff a sock, make sure it is too large to swallow. When the sock begins to fall apart, pick up the pieces and throw them out to avoid the complications of an obstructed digestive tract. Large, raw, meaty bones are also ideal teething items. After your puppy has his adult teeth, raw bones can help keep his teeth clean and give him some exercise and diversion.

Young pups are especially vulnerable to poison, so take care where you leave the pup unsupervised. Insecticide-treated baseboards have put more than one pup in emergency care. Cupboards left open are inviting and often dangerous. Think about puppy-proofing an area as you would for a child.

As with other potentially destructive habits, chewing may be an expression of boredom or frustration. The owner has a responsibility to recognize boredom and provide an outlet. One solution is to spend more play time with your pup. Another is to keep him in a crate with a toy when you cannot be around. A dog that does not have work to do will find another activity to replace it. If you are concerned about the appearance of your home and property, you should provide diversions for your dog before he decides to do the remodeling himself. Going for walks, jogging, obedience classes and supervised play with other dogs are logical activities in suburbia. If you are a jogger, do not take your young pup for very long outings. The distance can be increased as the pup grows and his bones are able to handle the exercise. If you have a canine daycare center in your area, consider enrolling your pup for short periods or while you are at work. That way he will have the benefit of socialization with all sorts of other dogs, plus exercise and play while you are not with him.

BARKING

Our own experience and that of others suggests that some livestock protection dogs can be nuisance barkers, especially in suburbia. A young pup might bark when he is left alone. Others will bay at a full moon or at a passing stray cat. These are, after all, traits common to most dogs. Some people believe that they should not correct a barking dog because that is what he is supposed to do to warn you of danger. They argue that such breeds should not be kept in situations where they are not allowed to bark. Most behavior experts agree that correcting a pup for barking out of frustration or insecurity will not affect his future ability to guard and warn of danger. It is preferable to remove the source of the frustration when possible. Before correcting him, make sure the pup is not barking at a legitimate danger. If the disturbance is a common occurrence, the pup should eventually learn to ignore it.

'Twas a dark and stormy night, and the livestock protection dog would not stop barking. Continual barking in the pouring rain off in one corner of the back yard while staring at the house was highly unusual behavior for this home companion dog. Normally she went out of her way to avoid getting cold, wet or muddy. After several minutes the owners grabbed flashlights, donned rain gear and ventured out to see what their dog was up to. On the other side of a hedge, their neighbor had suffered a heart attack and was lying on the ground, gasping for life.

One breeder, who usually had ten or more protection dogs around at any one time, had an unusual kennel tradition—the evening howl. Around sunset, the alpha dog began to bay. The others joined in and for about half a minute meaningful conversation was out of the question. We tried doing this at our farm. We would howl in a wolf-like manner, and yes, the dogs would join in. They did not, however, pick up the habit on their own, except to join in with the occasional emergency vehicle siren or howl back at a yipping pack of coyotes. We did, however, discover from this experiment that howling can be used to silence dogs. If you think loneliness, boredom or insecurity may be causes of your dog's barking, try having a howl with him. After a minute of vocalizing, he may be content to rest silently. One leading canine behaviorist suggests that you can train dogs to bark or howl on command, and eventually you should be able to turn the barking on or off. This type of control training can also be applied to dogs who jump (see below).

As a last resort, if usual methods for showing disapproval don't stop the barking, you may want to consider using an electronic collar. There are now electronic and other types of anti-bark collars that are effective and humane. Care should always be taken to use these collars as instructed by the manuals. A good collar will allow the dog a few "free" barks before issuing an audible warning—a buzz or a beep. If the dog continues to bark the collar will emit a shock or a spray of an obnoxious substance to interrupt his barking sequence. Most dogs figure out that when they are wearing the collar they cannot bark; without the collar they are still willing to vocalize.

DOGS THAT JUMP UP OR BEG

Jumping up on people and begging for food occur because owners allow this behavior. That cute little puppy will some day weigh 100 pounds or more. Also consider that he won't be able to distinguish between your play clothes and dress suit. Therefore, even little pups need to be taught not to jump up. To prevent jumping from becoming a habit, get your puppy to sit each time you first see him. Call him, ask him to sit, and only then praise, pet or give him a treat. If your pup has already developed the jumping habit, the traditional deterrent is to bump him in the chest with a raised knee as he is on the way up. If the pup is pawing at you or the furniture where you are sitting, some people try to discourage the behavior by pinching the skin between the toes with their fingernails. A squirt of water in the face from a water pistol or spray bottle can be effective, or for tougher dogs, a squirt of lemon juice from one of those lemon-shaped plastic containers. Finally, although probably this method should be tried first, teach your dog to jump up on command. The dog is rewarded for this behavior only when the jumping is solicited. Theoretically, the dog will not jump up without the command if he has been properly taught and reinforced.

Begging is easy enough to solve. Do not reward begging in the first place. If begging has already become a habit, ignoring the dog should eventually work. An older pup or dog can be put on a down/stay during mealtimes. The down/stay training technique is discussed in many of the referenced texts.

OBEDIENCE TRAINING—BEYOND BASIC COMMANDS

We highly recommend that anyone who owns a livestock protection dog as a companion attend obedience classes. Learning correct procedures for teaching various obedience exercises and obtaining canine and human socialization for your pet are essential if you and your dog are to get along in an urban society. The ultimate tests of obedience will occur in distracting circumstances, away from your home, usually when you aren't expecting them. If you want a companion that can accompany you without incident to strange places, expose him as a pup to as many stimuli as possible. These dogs are creatures of habit; if you establish the "habit" of traveling to new places, where the unexpected is likely to occur, your dog will accommodate change more readily.

Some people are interested in having attack-trained dogs for their personal protection. We have found that for livestock protection dogs this type of training is unnecessary—most of them will protect naturally because that is what they have been bred to do. Their protective nature is considered to be an extension of maternal or paternal instincts, and is based upon the formation of strong bonds. This is different from the trained aggression/protection taught at police-dog type schools or for Schutzhund competition. We believe that most livestock protection dogs are not ideal candidates for traditional attack training. Exceptions may include some Caucasian Ovcharkas and Kangal Dogs that have been trained and selected for police and military work in their native countries. Instructors of these programs have told us that they prefer to train biddable dogs who treat biting as a form of play, which can be quickly turned on or off by the handler. Livestock protection dogs are generally too serious

We sold a livestock protection dog as a companion to a woman years ago. She wrote about two years later to tell us this story. She loved her dog dearly and took him everywhere. Her neighbors loved her dog. He was totally loving and affectionate to everyone. He even lay down in the presence of cats instead of chasing them. He seemed to love everybody and anything, especially if it was young. The owner had come to the conclusion that her dog would never protect her, but adored him anyway. One day while jogging with her dog in a park a man pushed her into bushes beside the trail. Her always-friendly, ever-gentle livestock protection dog companion acted so quickly, the incident was over in seconds. The attacker let out a loud yelp, grabbed at his bitten buttock, and ran away. The dog sat beside his owner, and waited calmly for her to get up.

about their work, and also tend to be larger than most instructors are comfortable with.

Occasionally there will be a dog that does not seem to have a protective bone in his body. We have received letters from owners who had been convinced their dog wouldn't oppose any person's actions. However, the letters were written after an incident when they really needed their dog . . . and the dog came through with strong, instinctive protection. Some of these dogs appear to be so gentle and loving that unless challenged by a real threat their true protective nature may never be evident. Livestock protection dogs are also sensitive and intelligent enough that testing their defensive reactions with a setup or mock attack often does not work.

CHILDREN AND DOGS

Many people ask the question, "Is this breed good with children?" We tend to answer, "Maybe." Whether a dog is trustworthy with children will depend on the personality of the pup or dog, the children and the parents, and the amount of training and socialization the pup receives. Children should always be supervised with pups. They cannot be expected to control pups, and may even hurt them. Conversely, as pups grow older and bigger, they may inadvertently hurt the children during exuberant play or teething. What is even more worrisome are parents who expect the dog to babysit or entertain the children. With few exceptions, these dogs should not be left unsupervised with very young children. All puppies should be socialized to children of a variety of ages. They do not necessarily react to a two-year-old as they would to an eight-year-old or a teenager. Parents must practice their leadership exercises with the children present, and when possible, the children should participate in these exercises. Pups must learn to respect the children as they would adults.

There are particular times when parents or caretakers should be especially careful; at meals and during reproductive cycles. Even if a dog has been taught that the adult owner may remove his food, the dog may not respect a child who tries to take away his bone or play in his food dish. Or a child may drop some food and try to retrieve it at the same time the dog does. A bitch in heat may be more irritable than she normally would be; a stud dog separated from a bitch in heat may also be sharper and may snap at a child who gets between him and his girlfriend locked away in another

Children and puppies are a natural mix. Pups, like this Great Pyrenees, should be exposed to well-behaved children, but always supervised. Photo by Karen Justin.

room. Livestock protection dogs are large, have strong instincts for preservation and are protective. Some of these breeds display primitive traits. Children are usually lower in the hierarchy, no matter how much respect the parents command for themselves. Yes, these dogs can and do protect children in the family. But we tend to make too many assumptions about how our dogs have bonded to our children, and may erroneously assume human motivations and traits.

Children should be taught how to approach strange dogs, or not, especially if they are tied up. This Great Pyrenees is friendly and well socialized. Photo by David Sims.

Still, the family dog has been known to display uncanny behavior. For instance, we were told about a toddler who wandered out of her yard one day when the gate was accidentally left open. The girl headed down the sidewalk, followed by the family's Akbash Dog. As she approached the end of the block and was about to step off the curb onto the road, the dog circled in front and would not let her proceed. The child pushed and tried to get around the bitch, but she would not allow the little girl to budge. A passerby noticed them and was able to return the child to her yard, unharmed, just about the same time a worried mother realized they were missing.

Keep in mind that even if the family dog adores and is gentle with the children, you cannot assume he will see all children in the same light. Visiting children playing too roughly with his kids may be seen as a threat and may be "disciplined" by the dog. Adults must always supervise such interactions, especially if they have not socialized their pup to all the children in the neighborhood. Dogs, in particular livestock protection breeds, do not necessarily generalize the way we humans do.

MULTIPLE DOGS, OTHER SPECIES

What about mixing a livestock protection dog with other breeds in the household? When possible, begin with a pup that is introduced to the established dog pack. Livestock protection dogs can get along with other dogs and will often protect them against strange dogs and people. There has been a discussion of the optimal mix of sexes (Chapter Three), and although same sexes can get along, a difference in their hierarchy ranking is best, that is, one should be more dominant than the other. If the other breed is spayed or neutered, and smaller in size, that contributes to pack stability also. Livestock protection dogs are often the most dominant in a mix of other dog breeds, although there are many exceptions.

Livestock protection dogs can get along with cats, birds and other species, but as always, careful introductions and the monitoring of interactions for a long time are necessary to prevent disasters. There are a few species that livestock protection dogs do not naturally protect—birds, rodents, rabbits and sometimes cats fall into that category, so extra care must be taken when raising them together. Remember also that due to the nature of these breeds, there is always the possibility of re-directed aggression (see Chapter Seven), especially when a dog is cooped up in a house or small yard and cannot get out to deal with a perceived threat. The bunny sitting next to him at the window may become the victim of the frustrated protection dog that can't do his job and chase the intruder away.

Koza, a mature Akbash bitch, provides a warm nest for two kittens as she dries off from a wade in the pond. Photo by Cindy Mellom.

THE VERSATILE PROTECTION DOG

Individual dogs within the livestock protection breeds have proven to be amazingly versatile. Indeed, their feats may be limited only by their owners' imagination and initiative. There are many activities that can provide hours of fun for both dog and owner. We've included some suggestions you may wish to explore. If your dog has the aptitude, we think you will find that participating with your dog in these worthwhile endeavors will prove a valuable experience for both of you. You and your dog will establish a rapport that will enrich your relationship.

We've recommended that companion dogs attend obedience classes, both for the valuable lessons learned and to socialize the dog with other canines and people. If you and your dog enjoy the training classes, you may wish to enter the world of obedience competition. Obedience trials have grown tremendously in popularity and many people have found great fun and satisfaction in participating. The American Kennel Club (A.K.C.), the Canadian Kennel Club (C.K.C.) and the United Kennel Club (U.K.C.) all offer different obedience titles. For example, in A.K.C. trials, your dog may earn a Companion Dog (CD), Companion Dog Excellent (CDX) and Utility Dog (UD) degrees. A specified series of exercises is required for each level of competition. A complete set of the rules governing competition is available from each of these organizations. A variation on obedience trials is rally obedience, a more informal and active format. For those with rare breeds, national specialty clubs often hold obedience competitions with their shows. There are also some alternative clubs where non-recognized breeds are welcome to compete. Susan Bulanda's Canine Source Book (see Bibliography) lists many of these organizations.

Most livestock protection breeds do not excel at obedience trials due to the repetitive nature of the training. They can, however, participate in another type of testing which in the long run is far more valuable and rewarding—the Canine Good Citizen (CGC) Program. Set up by the A.K.C. to promote good relations between dog owners and the general public in the current atmosphere of anti-dog legislation, this program utilizes some of the lessons learned in obedience classes and applies them to everyday situations. As the A.K.C. puts it, "It identifies and rewards dogs that have the training and demeanor to be reliable family members as well as community members in good standing." Evaluators consider if each dog they are testing is one they would like to own, is safe with children, is welcome as a neighbor and makes his owner happy while not making someone else

Rudy the Malamute shows Arthur the Akbash pup a few wrestling moves. Exhausted by their play, they nap behind the puppy barrier. Photos by Deb Grady.

unhappy. The tests include accepting a friendly stranger, sitting politely for petting, appearance and grooming, going for a walk, walking through a crowd, obeying "sit" and "down" on command, staying in place, coming when called, reaction to another dog and to distractions (for example, shopping carts) and supervised separation. Obviously only well-socialized and well-trained dogs will pass this test. However, this provides a valid way to determine if your dog is a well-adjusted companion, and can certainly be a challenge for some dogs.

You may also wish to try your hand at tracking competition. Often, those who have participated find tracking to be one of the most rewarding exercises available. In tracking, the handler must rely on the dog's natural tracking ability. While you can teach your dog the basics of tracking, you cannot really train him, per se. Rather, you teach him to use his nose and the rest is up to him. Trials are judged on a pass or fail basis. Contact your local obedience club or one of the kennel clubs for information on this activity. Should your dog prove an exceptional tracker, you may wish to get in touch with some of the rescue organizations that are called upon in emergencies. We know of Komondorok that have been successfully used in mountain rescue work. However, search and rescue dogs need to be able to get along with other dogs and handlers, so obviously such dogs must be exceptionally well socialized.

Devotees of obedience are always searching for novel challenges. In recent years, many non-standard trials have been instituted. Some obedience clubs now offer scent hurdle racing and agility trials. Check with local obedience fans for information on these activities. Even if you choose not to participate, you'll enjoy watching the amazing feats performed by the dogs entered.

If you enjoy hiking, you may wish to bring your dog along. Physically, ⬚⬚⬚⬚ guardian breeds are particularly well suited to backpacking. ⬚⬚⬚ze and rugged constitutions, these breeds can be ideal ⬚⬚⬚ Most dogs can comfortably pack one-third of their ⬚⬚⬚ be evenly distributed on each side. Dog back- ⬚⬚⬚hased from supply houses catering to sled ⬚⬚⬚n some national parks and forests. Be sure ⬚⬚⬚g and heading for the wilds. The down- ⬚⬚⬚for a walk is that many livestock pro- ⬚⬚⬚ey have been very well socialized. ⬚⬚⬚ly react aggressively to strange ⬚⬚⬚ll have to determine if leaving

Agility exercises can be good fun and exercise for some dogs and owners. Photos by Diane Spisak.

your dog off lead will be safe, even in more remote areas. Some dogs can never be off leash.

In years past, weight pulling was considered the exclusive province of the larger sled dog breeds. In recent years, however, owners of large, strong dogs are discovering that this is a fun activity that their dogs may also enjoy. Check with a sled dog club to see if they permit other breeds to participate. The Canine Source Book lists clubs that hold weight pulls. During summer months, carting is another activity that dogs and owners can participate in. On an individual basis, there is no reason for those who live in winter conditions not to teach their dogs to pull toboggans and sleighs, or pull someone on cross-country skis for some ski-joring. With their large size, strong necks, chests and shoulders, the livestock guardian breeds would seem a natural for these activities. Keep in mind that not all of them are built to pull—the long-legged Akbash Dog does not usually have ideal conformation for this type of activity; they are built to run, not to pull.

For those breeds with a sighthound ancestry, such as the Akbash Dog, lure coursing may be another enjoyable activity. The lures are usually made of cloth and are attached to a fast-moving pulley. While you are likely to turn a few heads when you show up with a non-traditional breed, don't let that stop you.

In the past, at least one organization devoted to training dogs as aids for the physically disabled has promoted the use of livestock protection dogs. This came about because an individual dog proved to be particularly adept at the task of helping her owner in a wheelchair. This dog even won a prestigious award for her work. Over the last decade, however, very few livestock protection dogs have proven suitable for this work—out of the many that began training in the program, few graduated and succeeded in this field. Livestock protection breeds, by and large, are simply too independent and too protective to be easily controlled by children, elderly people, permissive owners or the physically disabled. These dogs respond best to people they respect. Even the average able-bodied pet owner has difficulty commanding the respect of these powerful, independent-minded dogs. Therefore, we cannot recommend that these breeds be used in such programs, allowing that there will always be exceptions, there will always be individual dogs that are not typical of their breed.

A variant of the service dog is the therapy dog. We know of a number of highly socialized livestock protection dogs that qualified to be taken into nursing homes and hospitals to visit the ill and incapacitated and bring a

Benek gets plenty of exercise hiking in nearby forests and on the beach.
Photos by Martine Dubuc.

little joy and excitement into their lives. These dogs and owners are usually part of well-organized therapy programs. They must first pass a series of tests, such as the Canine Good Citizen test described above, before being allowed into public institutions. Where they have done so, the results have been most rewarding for all involved.

If you do own a companion dog, we urge you to get out and have fun with him or her. If you are prepared to include your dog in all aspects of your family life, providing the essential training along the way, you will most likely have a well-adjusted, happy pet that is a joy to live with.

Zeki and Zanda, companion Akbash Dogs, each have their own beds. Photo by Huub Hendrix.

Diet and Its Many Influences

CHAPTER

10

Many of the essential points on diet have been discussed in earlier chapters. We would like to review some of the more important concepts, add a few new perspectives, and discuss diet as the central theme, instead of a peripheral issue.

Conventional wisdom suggests that the working dog will maintain a slim and healthy body. Experience has shown that indeed many will self-limit their food intake. However, our personal observation is that even working dogs are often overfed and a disturbingly high percentage are overweight and even obese. Not only does this shorten their lives and contribute to health problems such as cancer, arthritis and joint strain which can result in cruciate ligament injuries, but owners are wasting their money on food. Furthermore, many of the foods are inexpensive commercial brands which provide calories without optimal nutrition. There is now a swing back to the "old way" of feeding dogs, utilizing raw food when possible and supplementing the commercial diets with wholesome, fresh ingredients. Perhaps we should all take a cue from the wolves and coyotes trying to feast on our lambs. They know good food when they see it. Don't we owe it to our dogs to provide the best we can for them?

DETERMINING OPTIMUM BODY CONDITION

A typically active, adult livestock protection dog will have a lean appearance. In the smoother-coated dogs, the ribs may show slightly. The "waist" will be well defined. To tell if a dog is in good weight, run a hand against the rib cage without pressing hard. The ribs should be apparent to the touch. Also, the backbone and hip bones should be easy to feel without pressing hard. Another way to check for body fat is to press your thumb and

171

index finger deep into the neck just in front of the shoulder. When you pinch your thumb and finger together they should be no more than half an inch apart, otherwise the dog is overweight. Be aware that older dogs tend to carry more weight in that area. Finally, when looking down on top of the dog, there should be a tuck just behind the rib cage (the waist). The pelvis should be narrower than the chest and shoulders. This may be more difficult to see in a heavily coated dog.

An overweight dog will have a more filled-in waist and his ribs will not be as easy to feel beneath the fat. You may have difficulty feeling the tops of the back bones (vertebrae). The pinch of skin at the base of the neck will be over half an inch in thickness. A dog is considered obese when he is twenty percent over the ideal weight for his build (height, bone structure and muscling). Obese dogs statistically have a much shorter lifespan than dogs in trimmer form. They suffer from joint problems, elevated blood pressure, diabetes, and heart and liver problems. Even ten percent extra weight will shorten the life of a dog. A recently published study following a

This Polish Tatra, described as a typical male, is lean and trim beneath his heavy coat. Photo by Carol A. Wood.

group of dogs for fourteen years showed that dogs kept lean all their lives lived fifteen percent (two years) longer than their heavier (but not obese) littermates. This difference in lifespan increases if the dog was an overweight puppy as well. Allowing a dog to be overweight is not a kindness to the dog. Unfortunately, most people, including many veterinarians, do not recognize obesity in animals, and consider lean dogs to be malnourished. Some veterinarians report that informing owners that their dog is overweight offends many clients so they no longer offer that opinion. But the bottom line is that dogs kept on the thinner side will live longer, healthier lives.

On the other hand, a busy farmer might overlook the early stages of malnutrition. Excessive thinness, a dull, uneven coat, or listless behavior may signal inadequate nutrition. The food may have spoiled, may be nutritionally incomplete, or possibly the dog isn't getting enough of it for a variety of reasons.

A SENSIBLE APPROACH TO FEEDING

How often have you seen people make a fuss over their dog as he eats? You may know someone who rewards his dog for cleaning the bowl by giving him an even better tasting tidbit. How many dog owners at some time or other give their dogs spicy leftovers? These are examples of people rewarding their dogs for eating. That is, the dog is not just deriving the nutritional benefits from the food, he is being socially rewarded for eating. He will be tempted to associate eating, whether he needs to eat or not, with his owner's approval. That is the first step toward obesity and may result in a fussy eater. The dog may also learn to hold out for better food or may just keep eating until more interesting food arrives.

The ideal situation is to have a dog that eats only when he needs nourishment. If an owner does not reward the dog for eating, but rather treats eating as another incidental necessity of life, much like urination or defecation, the dog will probably be a better guardian and a healthier animal. The dog will be at an ideal weight and without a food obsession. How does one do this? The methods are simple. Choose a high-quality, balanced dog food that is nutritionally complete and made from wholesome ingredients. Whatever you choose, feed your dog once or twice each day, offering the food for about five to ten minutes each time. Do not be overly affectionate during feeding but, rather, go about other chores, leaving the dog

A young Komondor is cooling off after a walk through the pond. The tucked up waist shows his trim body condition. Photo by Lyn Bingham.

to eat on his own. Remove the leftover food without fanfare. In as little as five minutes, a mature dog can eat all he needs for a day. A young pup should be fed two or three times a day. Do not create a situation where the dog associates your affection with eating. Wait until you have removed the food bowl before you pet the dog or give him any extra form of attention. If a puppy does not learn to associate food with any form of reward other than a content stomach, he will not be likely to develop feeding problems later in life.

We do not recommend free-choice feeding where food is left for the dog to eat how much and when he pleases. First, food left out will lose its nutritional value due to exposure to the elements—air, light and heat. Dry dog food should be stored in a cool, dry place away from sunlight or kept frozen. Secondly, some dogs will overeat, grow too fast and be susceptible to joint problems such as osteochondrosis and hip dysplasia (see Chapter Eleven). From both the welfare and economical points of view, it makes little sense to let dogs eat free choice. Puppies fed a restricted but healthy diet will grow more slowly, their bones will have a chance to mature properly to support their adult weight, and they will attain their genetic potential.

A frequently asked question is what is a healthy weight for a pup at the different developmental stages? Each breed has a normal adult size range which is specified by the breed standard. For Akbash Dogs, the breed we are most familiar with, puppies are born weighing about one pound. By the first day of the third month most female puppies weigh between 25-30 pounds (11-14 kg) and most male puppies weigh 30-35 pounds (14-16 kg).

Table 1. Typical weights for male and female Akbash Puppies:

Months of Age	Females		Males	
	Pounds	Kilograms	Pounds	Kilograms
3	25-30	11-14	30-35	14-16
4	40-45	18-20	40-50	18-23
5	50-55	23-25	50-60	23-27
6	60-65	27-30	60-70	27-32

Table 2. Weights of mature Akbash dogs in lean, ideal body condition, with height taken at the shoulder:

Height		Females		Males	
Inches	Centimeters	Pounds	Kilograms	Pounds	Kilograms
26	66	65-80	30-36	80-90	36-41
27	69	70-90	32-41	85-95	39-43
28	71	80-100	36-45	90-100	41-45
29	74	85-105	39-48	95-110	43-50
30	76	90-110	41-50	100-115	45-52
31	79	90-115	41-52	100-125	45-57
32	81	–	–	105-130	48-59

They tend to add another ten pounds per month up to seven months or so. The heavier-boned, mastiff-type pups will tend to weigh more; the sighthound leaner body, finer-boned type will weigh less.

When someone brags to us that their Akbash Dog weighs 170 pounds, we can be quite certain that this dog is obese. Sadly, the last such dog we saw in this weight category died of cancer at an early age.

There are times when you need to increase the calories fed to your dog. Young puppies, bitches in the last half of pregnancy, lactating bitches and any dogs working extra hard at patrolling their territories require more calories. This is the time to increase the number of feedings per day as well as the energy density if you are using commercial dry food. If a specially formulated feed is not used, the regular chow should be supplemented with more fat, protein and carbohydrates such as yogurt, cottage cheese, meat and eggs. A high-quality puppy chow can meet the requirements of most lactating bitches, but supplements are recommended.

Sick dogs and older dogs may also require special diets. In these cases you may wish to consult with your veterinarian. A number of the references at the end of the book also provide information about special diets and feeding problems.

HOW TO SELECT THE BEST FOODS FOR YOUR DOG

In the past few years the concept of feeding whole raw foods to dogs has resurfaced. Proponents claim that this is the natural way of all canids—coyotes, wolves and feral dogs have survived on raw foods and carrion for millennia. Domestic dogs learned to depend on humans for their food, but when left to their own devices, they fell back to the old ways, hunting live game and eating berries, fruits, roots, vegetables and carrion. In fact, according to some theories, and most recently presented by the Coppingers in their book Dogs, dogs were domesticated from opportunistic wolf-type ancestors that hung around village garbage dumps and feasted on leavings. Commercially packaged dog foods are a relatively new invention, dating back less than sixty years. There are claims that the canine population has suffered from the inadequacies of

Swimming is another great exercise and activity for those dogs who like to get wet and paddle around. Kara the Aquabash. Photo by Orysia Dawydiak.

commercial diets as our nutritional scientists try to reproduce the "balanced" diet required for optimal health. In fact, most of the requirements for nutrients are based on determining the minimum amounts necessary to remain alive and produce normal body functions. The actual amounts of nutrients for "optimal" health are unknown.

The best approximation of a diet providing optimal health is the natural diet. The acronym "BARF" has been coined for the "Biologically Appropriate Raw Food" or "Bones And Raw Food" diet. It consists of, for instance, raw meaty bones, raw meat, fresh ground vegetables, raw eggs, yogurt and supplements such as kelp, cod liver or salmon oil, and ground flaxseed. There are a number of diets and recipes published (see Bibliography) and a growing number of enthusiastic proponents. They claim that many of the diseases that did not previously afflict the general canine population are due to the inadequacy of commercial diets, resulting in diminished immune systems. Time will tell if dogs fed such natural diets will, in the long term, be healthier than those remaining on less expensive commercial diets. This is a mass-scale, owner-driven experiment that is just getting started.

Since the concept made so much sense to us, we switched to the BARF diet a number of years ago. This diet does tend to be more expensive than most commercial dry diets, and takes more time to plan and prepare. Recently a number of enterprising individuals and companies have begun producing commercial versions of these raw diets, and this will certainly make feeding them more convenient. However, most of these commercial diets will remain impractical for many people since the food must usually be kept frozen or chilled, is not readily available everywhere, and is more expensive. A freeze-dried version of BARF has recently been added to the options available. For those who wish to "upgrade" their current feeding practices, we would suggest that they begin with a high-quality dry food (discussed below) and supplement whenever possible with fresh ingredients such as raw meat, raw meaty bones, yogurt, cottage cheese, eggs, etc.

Detractors of the BARF diets often cite cases where raw bones have caused problems for dogs. It is true that some dogs have problems digesting raw bones, and this can result in impacted bowels or bone fragments wedged in their mouths, for instance. If you wish to feed raw bones but are worried about problems, you can avoid these problems by only offering large joint or knuckle bones which the dogs cannot swallow. Another concern is that some dogs can become highly protective of their bones, and if there are a number of dogs around, there can be occasional fights. Large, fresh, raw bones are wonderful for keeping plaque from building up and providing some exercise and diversion, but not everyone will be able to feed them to their dogs. Each owner will have to determine if bones can be fed, what type, where, how and to what dog. Cooked bones, especially from poultry, should never be fed since they may splinter and cause internal hemorrhaging. Some of the commercial raw diets actually grind up bones to include in the mixture, so dogs will still get the benefit of the minerals but not have to chew them up. For more information on BARF, a number of books are listed in the Bibliography.

If you plan to feed a commercial dry food to your dogs, you should learn to evaluate the products available to you by reading the ingredients listed on the packages. Ingredients are listed by their weight contribution to the food: the first ingredient is found in the highest proportion, the second ingredient is next most abundant and so on. According to The Whole Dog Journal (February 2002), a monthly non-commercial consumer guide to caring for dogs, there are several hallmarks of a high-quality food. They include superior sources of protein, such as whole fresh meats or single-source meat meal such as chicken meal rather than

Magda, a Maremma/Sarplaninac cross lives with and protects Angora goats. The buck next to her is thirteen years old. Photo by Janis Moore.

poultry meal, a whole-meat source as one of the first two ingredients and whole, unprocessed grains, vegetables and other foods. Even better would be two meat sources such as chicken and chicken meal listed in the first three ingredients. If you see that there is only one meat source and a number of grains listed, it is likely that the percentage of grains is much higher than meat.

High-quality dry foods should also contain a minimum of food fragments and meat by-products. Food fragments are inexpensive by-products of other food manufacturing processes, such as brewer's rice, a waste product from alcohol production, and wheat bran. Also watch for products that contain several fragments of a single food, such as rice flour, rice bran and brewer's rice. Meat by-products should not form the main source of meat, but may show up lower in the list after other meat sources. Low-quality dry foods may contain the following ingredients: generic fats or proteins, artificial preservatives such as BHA, BHT or ethoxyquin, artificial colors, propylene glycol and sweeteners. Generic fats would be listed as "animal fat" and may be mixture of a variety of fats, such as recycled restaurant grease. A single-source fat such as "beef fat" is preferable. Likewise, "animal protein" is inferior to "beef protein" or "chicken protein." For a review of some of the best dog foods on the market, check out The Whole Dog Journal February issue each year.

Finally, a word of caution. Dogs should not be fed all-meat diets. Meat alone does not include all the vitamins, minerals and fats that dogs need to grow and be healthy.

THE DOG THAT WON'T EAT

If a dog goes off his feed for a prolonged period, he will probably stop being an effective guardian. There are many reasons why a dog might stop eating. Hormonal changes such as puberty, a bitch in heat nearby, or a new pregnancy can cause a temporary loss of appetite. Excessive heat can also reduce the desire for food. A hot dog will have to pant to cool down. Panting uses large amounts of water, so the dog becomes thirsty. In very warm weather, a high rate of drinking may keep the belly full, suppressing the appetite. A dog may also go off feed if he is ill, due to an infectious disease such as distemper or parvovirus or due to ingesting a noxious substance. If anything like this is suspected, a veterinarian should be consulted immediately.

THE DENTAL CHECKUP

Checking your dog's mouth (and the rest of his body, for that matter) is a sound, economical investment of your time. You could arrange to have a veterinarian come out to perform this service for you, but there is not much work involved.

The easiest way to look into the big mouth of a large guardian dog is by rolling him over onto his back. If you have been handling him frequently since he was a puppy, this should not be a problem. Offering to scratch his belly usually provides ample enticement. Then, while scratching around his neck and head, the upper lips can be flipped out of the way. It is also easy to open the jaw quite wide, though for only brief periods of time. Most problems within the mouth give themselves away by producing a foul smell, so your nose can be the first diagnostic indicator. If the gum around the base of any one tooth appears to be excessively reddened, there may be a problem developing underneath the gum line. If a tooth has excessive plaque developed around its base or if a tooth is noticeably off-color when compared to the others, there may be dental caries to worry about. If you ask, your veterinarian may teach you how to recognize and remove plaque. Otherwise, offer the dog fresh raw bones to chew to keep his teeth clean the natural way.

Livestock guardians face dangers that house pets would not encounter. A large animal, such as a cow or horse, may kick a dog and knock out or break a tooth. There is a reasonable possibility that a root canal infection could develop. Problems associated with an infected root canal may not become apparent for a long while after the original accident. We recommend that if you witness such a tooth fracture, you have your dog examined by a veterinarian. Some dogs have been known to chew rocks or chomp on metal fences and fence posts in frustration. If your dog is one of those, you should be examining his teeth regularly for problems.

Highly undershot or overshot bites are also implicated in a dog's problems with ingestion. If a dog has a bad bite, it may eventually lead to an uneven wearing of teeth and difficulty with chewing food properly. If your dog suffers in this way, be prepared to change the type of diet as the dog matures. The ideal bite is called the scissors bite, where the upper teeth (incisors and canines) close just in front of the lower teeth. However, a dog with slightly undershot jaws (the lower teeth close just in front of the upper teeth) or an even bite (incisors meeting) should not suffer much unusual wearing either. In an even bite, the incisors may wear down a bit earlier.

Health Problems

Livestock protection dogs are among the larger breeds of canines, sometimes classified as giant breeds. As such, they are subject to a number of maladies which occur in large dogs. These include canine bloat, hip dysplasia, osteochondrosis, panosteitis and cruciate ligament injuries. These problems have been chosen for inclusion in this text partly due to their severity, but more because they are poorly understood by many dog owners and there is a shortage of information readily available about them.

CANINE BLOAT

Also known as gastric dilatation, torsion or gastric volvulus, bloat is poorly understood. A number of dog food companies and veterinary research institutions currently sponsor research on this problem. Put simply, the stomach rapidly expands, twists, and may rupture and/or cause a fatal disruption of the blood supply. There have been a number of theories proposed to explain its occurrence. Veterinary researchers do not have enough evidence to present any of them as fact. All we can say is that a combination of events has been associated with most instances of gastric bloat. A dog that has just eaten a large meal, has consumed water rapidly, and exercised vigorously before or after the meal is predisposed to bloating. Most current veterinary articles on bloat suggest that if your dog has just eaten a large volume of food, you should not allow him to drink a great deal. Restrain the dog until some of the food has been digested. Do not feed your dog immediately after exercise. Also, do not allow an overheated, thirsty dog to gulp great quantities of water in a short time, whether or not a meal was just ingested.

Recently it has been shown that there is a correlation between certain conformational features of some dogs and a higher incidence of bloat. The ratio of body length to chest diameter may be different for dogs that are more likely to bloat. Lines of dogs predisposed to bloat were studied and measured. Some of the breeds involved included Standard Poodles, Golden Retrievers and Great Danes, all deep-chested breeds. The studies are incomplete but very interesting, since a number of livestock protection breeds are also deep-chested. However, not all deep-chested breeds are predisposed to this condition, so researchers are still trying to piece the puzzle together.

Other suggested causes of bloat that have yet to be substantiated include the composition of foodstuff that a dog eats and the presence of bacteria in the stomach. Certain components of dog food may cause enzymes to be overactive in the gut, producing gas at too great a rate for the gut to handle. At this time, the best preventive is to keep a dog quiet after a meal and not allow rapid drinking of water. If you know that a littermate or other relative of your dog has been affected by bloat, be especially aware of the possibility. Watch your dog for any unusual behavior after a meal or bout of drinking.

Signs of canine bloat include general agitation, pacing, unsuccessful attempts at vomiting and, perhaps, excessive salivation. If inspected more closely, a dog with bloat would show distension of the stomach and an increased heart rate. During bloat, the stomach is expanding, and, for reasons not yet known, the dog cannot belch, vomit or pass food into the intestine. As bloating continues, the stomach almost always begins to twist inside the abdominal cavity, rotating in such a way as to effectively close off the esophagus and intestine, twist shut local blood vessels and press up against the diaphragm. The net result of the twisting—which veterinarians call volvulus—is reduced return of blood to the heart, causing a more rapid but weaker pulse, difficulty breathing, shortage of blood to some parts of the abdominal organs and, eventually, shock. A dog in bloat requires veterinary assistance quickly. Unfortunately, many dogs do not survive their first episode with bloat. Those that do have a greatly increased risk of repeated bloat.

On a more optimistic note, canine bloat is not particularly common. It does tend to occur, however, in the larger breeds of dogs, and usually affects older dogs more often than younger ones unless they are predisposed to it. Therefore, we have introduced the topic so that you will be able to recognize its signs. Remember to ask a breeder from whom you are considering buying a puppy if there is a history of bloat in the bloodlines. Some owners who are aware that there is an incidence of bloat in the relatives of a pup opt to have the stomach tacked during a spay or neuter procedure, thereby preventing the possibility of the stomach twisting.

Having given warning about bloat, we have to add that we have seen our dogs break the anti-bloat rules many times with no ill effects. Are we just lucky? Maybe. In truth, too little is known about bloat at this time to permit definitive commentary.

HIP DYSPLASIA

Hip dysplasia (HD) literally means improper growth of the joint between the pelvis (hip) and the femur (thigh bone). The femur is the large bone that attaches to the hip, in a ball-and-socket type of joint. In actuality, the term hip dysplasia is used to describe a series of problems that center around that joint. Much of the long-term pain that results from hip dysplasia has more to do with improper wear in the joint, causing arthritis and the production of rough-edged bone around the joint. However, the overall process, which often ends up producing a dog that is lame, crippled or in pain, is hip dysplasia.

Hip dysplasia can be mild to severe. Some affected dogs will live long and active lives without requiring surgery, especially if they are supplemented with nutrients which aid in joint lubrication (for example, chondroitin and glucosamine sulfates). Regular chiropractic adjustments can also be beneficial by keeping the spine in alignment and reducing or preventing arthritis of the spine. More seriously affected dogs can have total hip replacements done or hip angles altered to relieve their symptoms and pain.

In severe cases, hip dysplasia can be recognized, radiographically, by eight weeks of age. Joint laxity (looseness of the joint) may be palpated by this age. However, a veterinarian could not pronounce hips sound at this early stage of bone growth, as dysplasia may set in later. In hip dysplasia, cartilage, which coats the articular or sliding surfaces of both the hip and femur, experiences unusual pressures. The cartilage surfaces become flattened, leading to a joint that is no longer a tight-fitting ball and socket. The edges of the hip bone socket become irritated by a subluxating (slipping) femur. Another consequence is the growth of extra bone along the edges of the joint, and the remodeling of the bone in the neck of the femur due to ligament stress. At this stage in the development of HD, a puppy would be experiencing

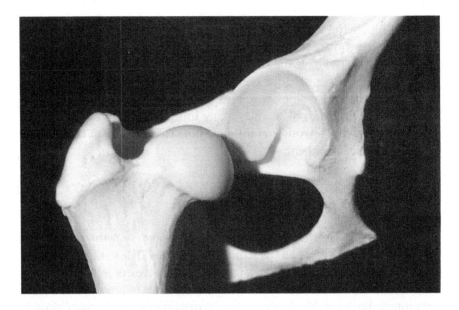

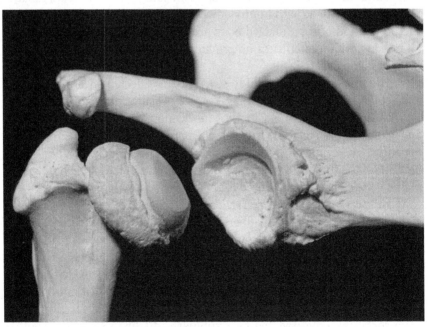

Top: A healthy hip joint. Notice the smooth surfaces.
Bottom: A severely dysplastic, remodeled hip joint. Notice the flattened, rough surfaces. Photos by Shelley Ebbett, Atlantic Veterinary College.

problems with the hip joint. The hip might just fatigue easily, but more likely it would be sore, requiring corrective adjustments of posture and manners of locomotion. Hip motion and length of stride are usually restricted. A dog with one sore hip will often sit crooked, with the sore side down.

In advanced hip dysplasia, we see bone remodeling, cartilage degeneration, and possible rupture of joint ligaments and the joint capsule. These changes result in a poorly defined hip joint, roughened, enlarged joint edges on both the hip and femur, and a series of secondary degenerative diseases, which will likely cripple the dog. Fortunately, there is relief available for dogs crippled by hip dysplasia. Most veterinary colleges, and some private veterinary practitioners, are able to replace defective canine hips with artificial substitutes.

Hip dysplasia is probably caused by genetic inheritance of poor hip structure, but nutritional and environmental factors also play a role in that they can either make the condition worse or help lessen the symptoms. For instance, an overweight dog is likely to suffer more pain due to the extra load he must carry. A responsible breeder will not breed dysplastic dogs and will guarantee against hip dysplasia. Should hip dysplasia occur in your puppy, you could minimize its development by restricting heavy use of the hip joint, supplementing with nutriceuticals, keeping the pup on the light side and slowing the rate of weight gain. Unfortunately, restricting exercise and access to food will not cure or prevent hip dysplasia. The genetic aspect of the disease is too overpowering.

On a brighter note, mildly dysplastic dogs can lead long and happy lives. Some remain active indefinitely. We recently watched a demonstration of police-trained German Shepherd Dogs. One of the police dogs was so dysplastic that he "bunny-hopped," moving both rear legs together instead of separately, in order to reduce the weight on each hip joint. Despite this problem, the dog appeared to be happy and performed all of his duties nearly as well as the other dogs. Many dysplastic dogs do not have to be euthanized or retired from protection duty. Dysplastic dogs, their parents and their littermates should not be used for breeding, though.

The Orthopedic Foundation for Animals, or OFA (University of Missouri-Columbia, Columbia, MO 65211 USA), provides skilled evaluations of canine hips for breeders or owners who are interested in reducing the incidence of HD in their breed. The OFA will evaluate radiographs from dogs of any age, but will only certify hips of dogs over two years old, an age beyond which HD is not likely to begin. The OFA also recommends that if either parent is dysplastic, or if any grandparents or a number of siblings or other close relatives have HD, the dog and his siblings not be used in a breeding program even if the hips are normal for those individual dogs. Some breed clubs insist that all their breeding stock have normal hips before registering offspring with full registration privileges. For more information about the OFA and its rating system, you may wish to consult with your veterinarian or check their website, www.offa.org.

The OFA publishes statistics on all breeds that have at least 100 evaluated dogs. The most recent review, which covers the years 1974 to 2001, lists the following livestock protection breeds and their incidence of HD.

Breed	# Evaluations	% Excellent	% Dysplastic
Great Pyrenees	4305	13.6	9.6
Akbash Dog	402	21.6	10.9
Anatolian Shepherd Dog	998	16.8	11.2
Tibetan Mastiff	476	5.7	11.6
Komondor	776	10.1	13.1
Kuvasz	1345	10.7	19.9

More recently, an alternative to OFA's method of evaluating canine hips has become available. Called PennHIP, this method was developed at the veterinary college of the University of Pennsylvania. PennHIP is a newer registry with a less-established track record. However, there are indications that PennHIP is a more sensitive test of canine hip dysplasia. If this is true, the PennHIP method may prove more useful for breed clubs and individual breeders who seek the best breeding dogs. The OFA examines the shape of the femur and hip's ball-and-socket type joint, looking at the smoothness and the fit of each bone. So does PennHIP, but with an additional variable. Joint laxity is looseness of the hip joint. If a hip joint is tight, meaning that the ball of the femur is not easily removed from the hip socket, there is a better chance the dog will not develop hip dysplasia. The PennHIP method includes a patented measurement of joint looseness or laxity.

Proponents of the PennHIP method of evaluation point out that using the OFA system alone has achieved too little improvement in North America's dogs, considering how long it has been in service and how many breed clubs have signed on. The OFA database is huge, but the results of using OFA data in breeding programs, according to PennHIP enthusiasts, have been unremarkable. A PennHIP evaluation of a dog's hips costs more money, but not enough to persuade anyone to accept one over the other method. PennHIP may eventually be recognized as the superior method for evaluating hips. For more information, consult with your veterinarian and/or visit www.vet.upenn.edu/research/centers/pennhip. While there are fairly specific instructions to veterinarians taking radiographs for OFA evaluation, the PennHIP registry will only consider radiographs and laxity data from PennHIP-certified veterinarians. You may have to search a little harder to find a veterinarian who is able to assist you in obtaining PennHIP certification.

OSTEOCHONDROSIS

Osteochondrosis (OC) is another joint problem that affects young, rapidly growing animals. It is most often seen in the shoulder joints of overweight male pups between six to ten months of age. Osteochondrosis also occurs in young humans, pigs, horses and even turkeys. OC can form in any weight-bearing joint of the body but most often occurs in the shoulder, stifle (knee) and elbow, and males are slightly more prone to develop OC than are females. Osteochondritis dissecans (OCD) is the condition arising from the disease process of osteochondrosis. The name is a Latin-based description of its characteristics: a dissection (dissecans) and inflammation (itis) of the cartilage (chondro) on bones (osteo). OCD occurs when cartilage, which forms the articular surface on bones that bear a significant portion of a moving dog's weight, is unable to maintain itself. As a result, the cartilage first thickens and then detaches, forming either a flap or a loose fragment in the joint cavity. The roughened part of the articular surface is extremely tender, leaving the dog lame.

Usually the outcome of OCD is far better than for hip dysplasia. Enforced rest, for several weeks to a month, often takes care of the problem. Cartilage fragments or flaps may dissolve and be resorbed. These fragments can also be surgically removed from the joint by a veterinarian. Thus, unlike hip dysplasia, OCD usually leaves no serious long-term effects.

OCD does, however, represent a debilitating condition which greatly worries owners and may result in a substantial veterinary bill. It is also painful for the dog, will prevent him from working, may interfere with bonding to livestock, and occasionally leads to permanent arthritis.

OC does not appear to be a genetic problem in the sense that hip dysplasia is. However, animals that are genetically programmed to grow rapidly are more likely to develop OC. The rapid gain of weight that precedes OC requires an abundance of food. Caloric intake is probably the most significant determinant of OC. Therefore, OC is an owner problem and a breeder problem. OC can be exacerbated by heavy exercise or continued exercise after the condition has set in. These factors, like the supplying of food, are owner-related considerations. A responsible breeder will inform a livestock protection dog buyer of the incidence of OC in the breed, but should not be expected to guarantee against its occurrence. To prevent OC, a buyer should limit the rate of growth of a puppy and young adult dog. Limiting the dog's rate of growth goes against the message in all those dog food ads we see on television and in glossy magazines. However, researchers have repeatedly shown that slowed growth sharply reduces the incidence of OC, without affecting the final size of mature dogs. If you are in doubt about selecting an optimal rate of feeding for a rapidly growing puppy, we recommend that you reread Chapter Ten for more details on feeding for healthy growth and development.

PANOSTEITIS

This condition is neither as common, nor as troublesome, as hip dysplasia or osteochondrosis. It is included here because its signs may trick an inexperienced person into suspecting such problems as dysplasia, OC, or bone fracture. Panosteitis gets its name from Greek (pan, the whole or an entirety) and Latin (os, bone; itis, inflammation). Panosteitis is an inflammation of entire bones, not joints. Panosteitis has occasionally been diagnosed in livestock protection dogs. The long leg bones of growing dogs are the most likely sites of panosteitis. The dominant sign is tenderness of an afflicted bone, sometimes to the extent that the dog will not put weight on the limb. In one veterinary study, panosteitis occurred in more than one bone at a time in over ninety percent of afflicted dogs. A dog will suddenly become lame and sore. The condition may remain for a week or two, then vanish. The bones involved may change over time. Cycles of lameness and recovery may be repeated. Of course, the recovery phases will always coincide with your veterinary appointments.

Accurate diagnosis requires the use of radiology. Panosteitis begins with an increase in the thickness of soft tissues around and inside bones. These changes lead to an actual increase in the thickness of bone tissue. The marrow cavity may become smaller in the process, and a veterinarian will look for a decrease in the sharpness of the edges of long bones in radiographs. The period of greatest pain seems to coincide with the stage of increasing soft tissue. Unfortunately, this stage is not conclusively detectable by radiograph or any other nonintrusive method. Only the more advanced stages of panosteitis show well on a radiograph. Panosteitis almost always goes away, whether or not medication is administered. Sometimes the marrow cavity of a bone is left slightly smaller, but usually the bones return to their normal condition.

Causes of panosteitis are not yet known. Bacteria do not seem to be involved. Other parts of the body, such as blood cell populations, are not affected. Panosteitis is probably not transmissible. Perhaps this is literally a case of growing pains in young animals that we, the owners, feed very well. Panosteitis appears most often in large, rapidly growing breeds.

CRUCIATE LIGAMENT INJURIES

Another problem of overweight dogs in combination with inadequate exercise, and possibly conformational factors, is the increased probability of ligament injuries. The most common problem is the tearing of cruciate ligaments. Cruciate ligaments stabilize the stifle (knee) joint. If you have ever watched dogs in play as they run, stop, twist and leap, it seems amazing they don't suffer more injuries than they do. Occasionally they will strain muscles as we all do when we overexert. The most problematic situation is the companion dog who is used to lying about at home, the pampered or even neglected pet. Busy owners, away at work most of the day and with many other things to occupy them, often don't provide their dogs with the exercise they need to stay fit. If companion dogs have large spaces to play in or patrol and other dogs to play with regularly, their self-administered exercise will likely increase. However, a "soft" dog that is taken out one weekend to roughhouse with another dog or has a visiting dog come over to play once in a while—especially one of those lightning-quick breeds like a Border Collie that can run circles around him—has a greater chance of over-twisting the stifle joint and tearing a ligament.

The odds for such an injury increase when the dog is overweight and may not have the most stable joints to begin with. There is some evidence that dogs with straighter stifles are more prone to cruciate tears. A veterinary orthopedic surgeon has told us that cruciate tears are most common in breeds like Rottweilers, Chow Chows and Golden Retrievers, in particular those with straighter stifle joints. There may also be a correlation between the relative length of the long bones (on either side of the stifle joint) which may predispose a dog to cruciate injuries. The tibia (bone below the stifle) should protrude just beyond the point of the buttocks when the dog is lying on his side, and the rear leg is bent as if the dog is sitting. The lower end of the tibia (the hock joint) should not be shorter than the point of the buttocks, nor appreciably longer. Either situation could create instability in the stifle. So if your dog appears to be straight through the stifle, or perhaps has an unusually long or short tibia, make an extra effort to keep him lean and fit. If that is not possible, monitor his play periods so he does not overexert himself. Cruciate repairs are expensive, take a very long time to heal while the dog must remain inactive, and will likely result in arthritic symptoms due to scar tissue buildup at the site of the injury. If you choose to let the tear heal on its own, this may result in heavy scarring with decreased mobility in that joint as the dog ages. The majority of cruciate tears we are aware of occurs in companion dogs, and this makes sense. Working dogs that patrol their pastures tend to stay more lean and fit, regardless of their conformation.

CHIROPRACTIC ADJUSTMENTS

Modern day human and animal chiropractic in the United States had its beginnings in the late nineteenth century. D. D. and J. J. Palmer of Davenport, Iowa, a father and son, started the first human chiropractic school which also included an animal hospital. One of the reasons for treating animals was to prove the theory of chiropractic and show how it worked without the placebo effect. Today animal chiropractic is becoming more widespread and is used as a complimentary modality with acupuncture and other forms of holistic medicine along with conventional veterinary medicine. Today chiropractors with or without veterinary degrees are certified internationally by the American Veterinary Chiropractic Association.

Active, trim working dogs like this Kangal Dog rarely suffer cruciate problems. Photo by Elisabeth von Buchwaldt.

There are certain situations where chiropractic adjustments may be useful. If a dog starts to pace instead of trot, cannot move in a straight line, fails to jump up to his normal spots, shows signs of leg weakness, has difficulty getting up, sits on one hip or holds one ear or eye higher than the other, he may be misaligned. Chiropractic cannot stop degeneration, but it can help the dog move more efficiently, and may slow any degenerative processes. It can also help with back conditions such as bulging discs, or lameness and in some cases paralysis. Other conditions which can be treated by chiropractic include urinary incontinence, lick granulomas and neck problems resulting from improper use of leashes or halters. We have seen the effects of veterinary chiropractic firsthand. Healthy, adult livestock protection dogs, apparently in peak physical condition, were examined and found to have irregularities in their vertebral alignment. After adjustment to correct the misalignment, the dogs reverted to lying on either side (something they had given up) and showed both increased energy and a calmer disposition.

ECHINOCOCCUS

There are many internal parasites which infect dogs. Some of them are debilitating, while others don't cause any particular harm. One, however, a genus of tapeworm called Echinococcus is becoming more prevalent in North America. It infects dogs, but the main concern is for human health—this parasite can kill people.

Echinococcus requires both a herbivore (for example, sheep, cattle) intermediate host and a canine definitive host to complete its life cycle. Having dogs on a sheep farm is bringing together the two ideal hosts for Echinococci. Other animals, including cattle, llamas, swine, goats and horses, can also serve as intermediate hosts, as can humans. Eggs of Echinococcus species are passed from a dog's feces to the ground or grass growing near the feces. Usually intermediate hosts become infected when they eat the contaminated grass. In the case of humans, touching the fur of dogs with Echinococcus eggs, being licked by a dog that has licked its anal region, or handling infected feces and then placing your hands near or in your mouth can lead to infection.

Echinococci don't present much of a threat to dogs. Even if they are infected, dogs continue to do well, and can accommodate heavy infections without any outward signs. However, Echinococci can seriously injure or even kill humans. Humans lack the defense mechanisms that other hosts have developed against Echinococci. If you read or hear about hydatid cysts, hydatid disease, Echinococcosis or hydatidosis, you are dealing with the effects of Echinococci. So many Australians were suffering from Echinococcus infections several decades ago that the government had to organize an expensive, nationwide eradication program. The Australian program required that government inspectors de-worm every farm dog or witness the administration of worming medicine. Unfortunately, Australians will always have an Echinococcus problem, and will always have to be careful about this tapeworm. In North America, the incidence of Echinococcus infections in humans is not high, but it is on the rise, particularly in the western Canadian provinces and American states, and in Alaska.

Echinococcus eggs are hard to detect in a canine stool sample, mainly because they look like the eggs of other tapeworms. They are not completely killed by the more common tapeworm medicines, either. Medicines may have to be specially ordered by a veterinarian, should you have reason to suspect Echinococcus infection. Imported livestock protection dogs should be shampooed thoroughly upon arrival to remove any Echinococcus eggs that may be attached to the fur. Parasitologists recommend that all dogs brought onto a property be shampooed and cleaned as if they are carrying Echinococcus. Provide Echinococcus-specific de-worming medicine immediately, and pay extra attention to your own hygiene. Thoroughly wash hands and clothes that have come into contact with a new dog. Prompt removal of dead livestock from your property will also help to minimize spread of Echinoccoci and other harmful agents. There are also wildlife hosts which can complicate management plans to eradicate the problem, should it occur in your area. If additional information on this topic is desired, the best sources are your veterinarian, a veterinary college, a community health nurse or doctor, the local library or, perhaps, the internet.

COAT AND SKIN PROBLEMS

Livestock protection breeds tend to have thick coats of fur, especially in the colder seasons and climates. Dogs that spend a great deal of their time outdoors or that live in areas with burrs and thistles should be checked periodically for thorns in their coats. Thorns, burrs and foxtails can work their way under the skin and cause abscesses. Komondorok have especially thick, tangled coats, which are often corded into long, dense "ringlets." Check the eyes of these dogs regularly. Determine that they are able to see through their fur and that their eyes are free of contact by hair or other particles. To avoid these problems, many ranchers routinely shear the coats of their Komondorok and even some Great Pyrenees in the summer months.

In the heat of summer, particularly in humid climates, dogs may develop skin problems, or they may become sensitized to fleas. Part the hair and look at the belly and around the base of the tail for signs of redness. Consult your veterinarian if you are unsure of any unusual colors or rashes on the skin. Extreme heat, especially in combination with high humidity, can be a serious problem for the active livestock protection dog. Heatstroke can occur in dogs and has claimed lives in the past. Clipping the coat and/or frequent brushing may be the best solution. Shorter-haired dogs with less dense coats are usually a better choice in hot climates. Do not be surprised or disappointed if your protection dog spends most of the hot sunny hours stretched out on the ground, digging a cool hole or seeking shade. Those same heat conditions will usually keep coyotes and marauding dogs away, too. Keep water, cool if possible, available at all

A full coat protects this Komondor from winter blasts. Photo by Lyn Bingham.

times, and provide shade if you can. If your protection dog is immobile from the heat, chances are that your stock is not very active either and will not be moving much.

ANESTHESIA

Large, deep-chested breeds, which includes most livestock protection dogs, are often more sensitive to anesthesia than other types of dogs. If you should ever have the occasion to take your dog to the veterinarian and there is a possibility that the dog may be anesthetized, ask the veterinarians and their technicians to be especially careful. These large dogs may actually require less anesthetic than their size would suggest. They may react more like the sighthounds than other breeds. Akbash Dogs and Maremmas may be particularly easy to overdose with anesthetic.

PROBLEMS WITH EYES AND EYELIDS

Inverted eyelids, a condition called entropion, is a problem in some breeds. Breeds such as the Chow Chow and Chinese Shar Pei are noted for this problem and corrective surgery is the rule. Entropion can occur during growth as a transient problem in any breed, large or small. However, if it persists for longer than a few weeks, there can be permanent damage to the cornea, which is being constantly abraded by the turned-in eyelashes. Surgery may be done at any time, from as early as six weeks of age to several months, if the condition persists. Since some forms of entropion are considered heritable, affected pups should not be used for breeding.

A clipped Great Pyrenees tolerates the heat of summer as he stands among his shorn flock-mates. Photo by Orysia Dawydiak.

Heritable entropion often occurs in both eyes at once. If only one eye is entropic, trauma to the eye and eyelid such as a poke by a stick or branch may be the cause.

Ectropion, where the eyelids are everted, is less common among the livestock protection breeds, but it does occur, usually in dogs with excessive skin or a relatively small eyeball compared to eyelid. Again, it can be corrected fairly easily with surgery, but the dog should not be used for breeding.

Livestock protection dogs are susceptible to the same problems that other dogs can experience. We have mentioned only a few of the maladies that may affect your dog. Certain breeds or strains may also suffer from inherited diseases and conditions. The Bibliography lists sources that list such inherited problems in the various breeds. Rabies, parvovirus, distemper and a host of other problems are covered in general dog care books, so they have not been included here. We have written this chapter with the idea that you will be a more knowledgeable and responsible owner/handler for having read it, but please don't consider this overview of problems to be comprehensive or complete. Chances are your dog will remain healthy if you provide a proper environment, pay attention to diet, health checks, de-worming and immunizations, and seek prompt attention for any problems that do arise.

An unconcerned (and perhaps tired?) mother lies by while Trooper, a two-year-old Kuvasz, meets her thirty-minute-old cria. Photo by Stuart Prisk.

Special Considerations for Unusual Livestock

Since the first edition of this book was written in the late 1980s, the variety of species guarded by livestock protection dogs has expanded. Today many of these animals are not considered particularly "unusual" but since they are beyond the realm of the traditional, we will categorize them as such. They include camelids such as llamas and alpacas, ratites such as ostriches, emus and rheas, and of course poultry—chickens, turkeys, peafowl, ducks and geese. There are likely other types of stock we could list; however, these are the most typical of the unusual. These animals can vary substantially in their behavior from the sheep, goats and cattle we are most familiar with, and often management and husbandry practices are unique, so that new challenges are presented when adding a livestock protection dog to the equation.

Although these unusual species can provide the livestock guardian and owner with additional challenges, many of the training principles are the same as for traditional livestock. When selecting a pup, care should be taken to match the pup with the type of stock, the management of that stock and the area the dog will have to cover. No doubt there will be other species that will be guarded by livestock protection dogs in the future. We have yet to test the limits of these versatile dogs.

POULTRY

Poultry are among the smallest of all species guarded by livestock protection dogs. They can also be among the most enticing for young pups to chase. Some dogs, not properly socialized to poultry, have been known to treat them like varmints that need to be exterminated. Most of the dogs we know will readily chase and kill mice, rats, gophers, rabbits, squirrels and even skunks. They must be taught that captive birds are part of the owner's domain and must be protected, or at the very least, left alone.

How does one start? Whether you are beginning with a pup or an older dog, you must be prepared to monitor the pup's behavior around the poultry at all times. Take the pup with you when you go out to feed and water and work with the flock. Initially you may have to keep him on lead, especially if the poultry are not used to a dog and are nervous in his presence. Birds will flap, squawk, fly or run, which is a stimulus for many pups to chase and join in the fun. If the pup shows any inclination to do so, immediately stop him by yelling something like, "Leave it!" or "Arrgh!" If the pup turns away from the birds, praise him, give him toys to play with or other diversions. If the pup continues to chase or shows interest in doing so, roll him onto his side or back and repeat your reprimand strongly, keeping him firmly pinned down. Some owners like to hold onto the muzzle while pinning the pup and reprimanding; others will grab them by the scruff roughly before rolling them over. The strength of your correction must suit the temperament of the pup—some are very sensitive whereas others repeatedly seem to miss the message. They will make the connection if you persist and are able to match the determination of the pup with an adequate reprimand. In the worst cases, pups may require strong physical discipline, such as grabbing the pup roughly by the scruff, lifting just off the ground, and then releasing or rolling him over and pinning him to the ground.

For older pups or dogs that are left with the birds unsupervised where the owner can spy on them unobserved, an electric collar can be used for

A mature Anatolian Shepherd Dog watches over a flock of birds. Photo by Jennifer Floyd.

immediate, long-distance corrections. Timing is critical in order for the dog to make the association between what he is doing and the correction, whether you are right there with him or watching him from your kitchen window. You must repeat this sequence as often as it takes. Most pups will stop chasing for the time being, but you should be prepared to interrupt this behavior every day until it is completely extinguished. During the training period, one poultry owner verbally reprimands her pups for even looking at the chickens while they are in the pen with the birds.

If you have a bird who is not afraid of the pup, so much the better. You can let that bird find occasion to peck at the pup, or you can set up the situation where the pup is allowed to investigate a chicken you are holding that may peck at him when he gets too close. Broody hens setting on nests tend to be more assertive and will often peck an inquisitive nose, as will mother hens with small chicks should the pup get too close. However you cannot depend on your chickens to discipline your pup—you must always be prepared to grab the pup before he can get too carried away in a play-chase and do damage to the birds. Even slapping a big paw down could flatten a tiny chick. Once pups learn the joy of chase, play and perhaps kill, it is much more difficult to dissuade them from that self-rewarding behavior, although it can be done.

The process can take longer if the poultry are not used to a dog. Be prepared not to trust your young guardian until he is twelve to eighteen months old or even older. Just as with sheep, the big mistake many dog

A goosed Akbash pup learns to respect birds with pinching beaks and bossy dispositions. Photo by Marsha Peterson.

owners make is to assume their dog is stock-safe when he isn't. A young dog will need an outlet for all his energy and playfulness, so you should also find ways to let him get his exercise. If you have other dogs that he can play with away from the flock, that would be ideal. Otherwise, you will have to be the playmate. And you can certainly encourage your pup to chase and destroy the real varmints when they show up.

Another consideration is that some dogs will learn to eat any eggs they find. This should be discouraged for a number of reasons, one being a health problem if a large number of eggs are ingested. Eggs contain avidin and vitamin A, which in high quantities can interfere with blood clotting and can be toxic, respectively. But further, some dogs will not differentiate between eggs and newly hatched, unfeathered chicks. Even dogs who don't eat eggs may not recognize newly hatched chicks as "real chickens" until they have grown feathers, so special attention must be paid to the interaction of the dog with hatchlings.

Many livestock guardian dogs instinctively guard against winged predators, such as hawks, owls and eagles. People who keep poultry but can't cover the yard with netting may find such predators swooping down to pick off chicks and the smaller bantam birds. This is a case where a well-trained, trustworthy livestock guardian can be worth his weight in gold. The dogs will also keep a variety of other predators out, from rats, racoons, skunks and snakes to foxes, coyotes, cougars and stray dogs who would love a chicken or duck dinner. Even human predators have been put to a run by these vigilant guardians.

As an added bonus, one Anatolian Shepherd owner reports that her dogs will break up fights between her birds. They also alert her to unusual happenings, such as a rooster tangled in his tether, or a baby chick on the wrong side of the fence or a bird in distress. As an aside, and considering another unusual species, we know of a mink rancher who uses Akbash Dogs to guard his property and the mink. The dogs will alert him whenever a baby kit has fallen out of his cage into the muck below. Occasionally they help round up loose mink, although they have also been known to play games of chase and be chased. No self-preserving dog would really want to tangle with a full-grown mink anyway.

One more word of caution. There are some species or individuals, notably large turkeys like the bronze-breasted turkey and some geese, that can be highly aggressive towards dogs. We have had reports of turkeys, male and female, harassing dogs, jumping on them and digging in with sharp claws, twisting the dog's skin in their beaks. We had one fearless gander who drove one of our Akbash Dogs out of the pen where she was left to guard their eggs from jays. The gander didn't protect the eggs from marauding birds, but neither would he tolerate the dog anywhere near him and his mate. We gave up—the jays won that round. Please don't reprimand your dog if he is being attacked by the birds and can't do his job.

RATITES—OSTRICHES, EMUS AND RHEAS

These big, flightless birds have gained in popularity over the past decade as a new type of livestock. Although their numbers have fluctuated wildly as speculators anticipated great profits and then learned that perhaps the market wasn't quite ready or well enough developed, it seems that some producers are prepared to stay for the long haul as they expand markets for some of the unusual by-products. For a time these birds were so valuable that a few farmers were using armed guards to prevent theft of breeding stock. They began to inquire about the use of guard dogs, but found that conventional guard dogs were too active and aggressive and tended to spook the birds, which could easily injure and kill themselves when frightened into running.

Even the traditional livestock protection breeds could not always be kept with ratites. Male ostriches during breeding season could and would easily disembowel a dog with their powerful forward thrusting legs and claws. Due to their size and behavior, perimeter fencing was devised such that guard dogs could patrol just outside the ostrich pens, but would remain nearby. Since the dogs do not really bond to big birds in such situations, they function more as territorial guardians. Ideally you should select guard dogs with lower activity levels who are less likely to startle the ostriches as they patrol.

Emu and rhea are smaller and less dangerous species and can tolerate the presence of livestock protection dogs inside their pens. They can still kick and peck at dogs; however, they are not likely to do as much damage, and most dogs can learn to avoid harm and even tolerate the pecking. Pecking is not necessarily an act of aggression with ratites, which will use their beaks to explore when they are curious. Some dogs will bond to the birds, and they are definitely protective. Like poultry, care has to be taken around ratite chicks and any puppy play-chasing should be discouraged quickly. The same training techniques would apply around young emus and rheas. However, older and mature birds can also

Top: An adult Akbash Dog with emu pal, Big Bird. Middle: Big Bird uses an inquisitive beak to explore the puppies. Bottom: Adolescent dog rolls over submissively for emu chick. Photos by Marsha Peterson.

Natasha, a six-month-old Akbash Dog, already expresses her maternal nature with these young emu chicks. Photo by Donna Hatcher.

be startled into running by a playful dog looking for some fun. Most livestock protection dogs will not be trustworthy around ratites until they are over a year of age. If you think your dog is ready to stay in with them full-time, make sure you can monitor him initially so you can correct him if he does decide to chase.

Livestock protection dogs are not as likely to chase older emus and rheas as they are other, smaller stock. However you should watch for irritable dogs that may snap at the birds. If a dog happens to connect with the small, vulnerable head, he can easily kill an emu or rhea. This type of "accident" can occur if the dog tends to get frustrated at fencelines (for example, sees something on the other side he'd like to get to but can't), if it is a bitch in heat or if it is a stud dog and there is a cycling bitch nearby.

LLAMAS AND ALPACAS

Llamas and alpacas are ruminants like sheep and cattle, so you might wonder why they should be any different than the traditional livestock to guard. In fact, all the training advice for sheep does apply to these camelids as well, but they do have a few unique features worth mentioning. First of all, llamas are actually used by some sheep and goat farmers to guard their stock. Certain neutered male llamas can be quite aggressive towards strange canines, and will go out of their way to drive them off by kicking, pounding and biting them. Due to their size they are

Akbash Dog Sharbat interacts with her alpacas. Sharbat saved this little cria's life when, at the age of four days, he was abandoned during a torrential downpour. She stayed with the cria and alerted the owners. Photo by Judith Sims-Barlow.

not considered as vulnerable as sheep or goats to begin with. However, not all llamas are aggressive towards canines, and there are predators which even the toughest llama cannot deter or fight against. These include cougars, grizzly bears, wolves and even a determined pack of coyotes or dogs. Coyotes have been changing their strategies lately, and have learned to hunt cooperatively. They have even been known to send out decoys to draw the guard animal away from the flock so the rest of the pack can attack from behind. In the areas where tough predators abound, llamas still need canine protection.

Alpacas are smaller than llamas and are more vulnerable, although there are also individuals that may not be particularly dog-friendly.

These tend to be males, and just as with rams and buck goats, some of these boys can be hard on protection dogs. We have heard many stories of how a male alpaca has harassed the guard dog, following him around, pawing him, sometimes jumping on him or even nipping the dog. Some dogs will submit and just try to keep their distance. However, it is not fair to the dog to force him to remain with this type of animal, and eventually the dog may begin to defend himself and get soured on all the stock, females and babies alike. Watch for this type of behavior and take corrective action by removing the aggressive animal or putting the dog with a friendlier group. If you are raising a pup and he is not ready to be left with younger animals, you will have to keep him in an area where he cannot be harassed by older stock. Knowing which animals you can leave your pup with is a balancing act—they need to be individuals that will tolerate or even like the pup, but that cannot be bullied by the pup or might even give the pup gentle corrections if he becomes too rambunctious. It may take trial and error to locate this individual or group of animals, but if you do not have anything available, the pup may have to remain in a pen next to the herd until he is old enough and trustworthy enough to be allowed in with them.

Great Pyrenees with a young alpaca. Photo by Tawny Bott.

One of the difficulties reported to us by alpaca owners is that young protection dogs often engage in wool-pulling. This seems to occur more frequently with alpacas than with sheep. Whether it is the soft texture of the alpaca wool, the lovely "feel" in the mouth, the fact that alpacas may tolerate this activity, or the playful behavior of alpacas that entices dogs to romp with them, we do not know. Wool-pulling may be more problematic with an "only" dog who has no other outlet for his exercise. Try to look at the situation from the dog's perspective. He can become bored hanging out with these woolly creatures day after day, especially if there aren't enough predators to chase off or bark at, and if the pens or pastures they live in are too small. Many livestock protection breeds are geared to patrolling tens and hundreds of acres. Living in a one- or two-acre enclosure can be highly frustrating for some dogs. Temporary solutions to play-chase behavior and wool-pulling include the use of drags or basket muzzles, but in the long run, the dog must be taught not to chase or pull wool.

Anatolian Shepherd Dogs with miniature horse foals. Photo by Henry Ballester.

Breeding

CHAPTER

13

You have a beautiful bitch, she guards your goats day in and day out, has hardly given you any trouble over the past three years, and many people have remarked they would love to have a puppy of hers. You paid $600 for her, and by now you've put in at least another $1500 with food bills, fencing supplies, veterinary expenses—why not get your money back, and then some? Why, she could have ten puppies; that would be $6000!

Stop right there. This simple calculation of profits is totally deceiving. We've bred dogs for over two decades and most years we were lucky if the dogs paid for themselves. In good years we earn a modest profit if you don't factor in an hourly wage for labor. The hours are long and the rewards often come mixed with failures. If you want to be a good breeder, you will not make very much money breeding livestock protection dogs. Your motivation should be to improve the breed and to produce excellent dogs that other people will value for their fine working qualities. If you have great dogs to start with, good animal and people management skills, and support from your breed club and working dog group, if you are prepared to put in a lot of time and hard work and have money to support this hobby, you may come out ahead financially. However, if making money is an essential goal, you are better off with a strictly show or companion breed of dog.

Let's say you feel that you do qualify as a potentially good breeder. Here are a few more questions to ask yourself:

1. Am I prepared to spend money on advertising well in advance of planning the litter, and do I have the money in reserve in case there are medical emergencies?
2. Have my breeding dogs been tested or screened for heritable defects common to the breed?

This ranch-raised litter of Akbash Dogs have their very own sheepskin bedding. Photo by Roman Kneblewski.

3. Am I familiar with the pedigree of the potential sire and dam, and the strengths and weaknesses of their ancestors?
4. Are the sire and dam reliable working dogs? Are their parents?
5. Do I have truly excellent homes if my bitch produces ten or more puppies?
6. Am I prepared to keep, train and socialize a number of pups if they cannot be placed right away, and can I afford to feed a huge, fast-growing litter of large breed pups?
7. Am I comfortable with my level of knowledge of canine reproduction, whelping and care of pups, nutritional needs and possible health problems?
8. Are there other dog breeders who would be willing to act as mentors to help me through this process the first time?
9. Am I willing to euthanize any pups with serious defects at birth?
10. Do I have a complete guarantee on my pups and am I willing to take back or help place any dog that my buyers no longer wish to keep?

11. Do I have a good information and support packet to give to my puppy buyers, and am I able and willing to help my buyers with training problems?
12. Am I prepared to ship pups by air if necessary, and do I know how to arrange this?

You get the idea. There is a lot to think about when planning a litter. There are books written about canine reproduction so we will not dwell upon that here. We will touch on some main points, and expand on a few ideas we think are particularly important with livestock protection breeds. A sample of a prospective customer questionnaire is included in this chapter and a puppy guarantee can be found in Chapter Three.

BREEDING STOCK

All breeding stock must have a good working temperament, be sound and have a conformation which meets the official breed standard. Without these criteria, there is no point in reproducing the dogs. You must be objective when evaluating a dog's breeding potential. This can be difficult to do at times, especially when you have an emotional attachment to your dog. He may be a wonderful sheep guardian, but if he is dysplastic you must not use him for breeding. He may be a gorgeous specimen but would rather play with and harass livestock than guard them. Find someone familiar with the breed and its working qualities to evaluate your dogs from an objective, unemotional perspective. Avoid what is often called "kennel blindness" when you are selecting breeding pairs.

We believe that if you wish to produce pups that will be working as livestock protection dogs, the parents of your pups should be proven working dogs also. There are cases where non-proven dogs do produce fine working pups, especially if they come from a long line of working dogs. Occasionally they are imported from their countries of origin and the owners know the dogs have a working pedigree, but are unable to raise them with stock. However, unless you are dealing with a rare breed, there is no compelling reason why you should be producing pups for livestock protection if your breeding stock have never seen sheep. How do you really know they have the aptitude to be stock guardians?

All breeding stock should have their hips certified free of hip dysplasia by the OFA or PennHip (see Chapter Eleven). Eyes can be tested by the Canine Eye Registry Foundation (CERF). If there are other tests you can do based on heritable problems in your breed, you should have them done. This will certainly make you feel better about offering a substantive guarantee, and buyers will be more confident in your dogs. Two dogs with excellent hip conformation can still produce a dysplastic puppy, but the odds are greatly reduced.

MANAGING BREEDING DOGS

If you own both the bitch and stud, your stud dog will usually let you know when your bitch is cycling and receptive for breeding. There are some bitches who are particular about stud dogs and this can be a problem if you have to take her to a stud she does not know. We have read that livestock protection dogs may have low libido, but this has never been verified by anyone we know. If you do not have a stud dog on your property, you may have to test the bitch (urine or blood samples) to know exactly when she is ovulating.

We have discussed elsewhere some of the drawbacks of keeping intact working dogs. When you are not breeding, you need to keep the bitch and dog apart during heat cycles. You should have a safe kennel where the bitch can be kept for up to three weeks. During that time the stud dog may drive you mad by howling, trying to escape to get to the bitch and generally being harder to handle. Breeders have reported being bitten while trying to handle frustrated stud dogs. If the bitches are kept with their stock, they may be more irritable and snap at animals they normally would leave alone. They may also be less interested in guarding, and may even attract strange male dogs onto your property. Be prepared for a thorough testing of your gates, fences and other confinement systems if you elect to keep intact livestock protection dogs on your property.

Breeders have different management schemes when it comes to breeding and calculating due dates. We allow the stud dog to breed the bitch only when we are around so we know the time and date of the first breeding. Counting from the day we first notice the bitch spotting blood, mating can occur between ten to seventeen days later. We wait a day and a half before allowing the two to breed a second time, then another day and a half if breeding is repeated. After that we let them remain together if they normally work as a pair. Generally, counting from the day of first breeding, pups are born sixty-one to sixty-three days later.

THE BRED BITCH AND WHELPING

Approximately two weeks after the first mating, we often notice a decline in the bitch's appetite. We liken it to morning sickness in pregnant women, and take it as a sign that she is indeed bred. The appetite of the pregnant bitch really begins to pick up at about week five or six. She should be offered as much high-quality puppy chow or her raw food diet as she wants to eat, unless she is actually getting fat. Toward the end of the pregnancy, she should be fed smaller but more frequent meals since there may be pressure on her stomach, especially if she has a large litter. Just before whelping, many bitches will refuse to eat. They also begin to look for a whelping area, often frantically digging deep dens under buildings if allowed to. Many working dog bitches are only comfortable whelping outside or near the barn if that is where they are normally kept. If the weather is too cold, we allow the bitch to have her first pup outside, and then we bring her and the pup into a warmer area where she can finish whelping. Newborn pups cannot regulate their body temperatures and need to be kept warm. Sometimes the dam can warm the pups on her own; we prefer to help her out a little. A word of caution here: Moving certain bitches in the process of whelping might interrupt the process and cause them to stop whelping altogether. This could result in the necessity for a C-section. If you are in doubt, try to keep her in a location where she can safely whelp, and use heat lamps or a heating pad if hypothermia is possible.

New mothers sometimes make mistakes, which is why we like to be around to supervise whelping. We find they are very good at removing afterbirth, cleaning up the pups, getting them to breathe and biting the umbilical cord at just the right place. Sometimes, however, they smother pups in their attentiveness to the latest pup being whelped. There were sixteen pups in our largest litter—no wonder mom lost track! A properly designed whelping box has four sides with a deep lip on all sides so pups can be pushed under the lip but not get squashed. We like to make sure that there is milk let down to begin with, that all the pups are on the nipples and nursing, and that there are no pups lodged in the birth canal that may need assistance.

There are so many potential complications in the whelping process, we are amazed when all goes smoothly. Fortunately, we've had very little trouble over the years. With the largest litters and with older bitches, there can occasionally be uterine inertia, a situation where it takes a very long time for all the puppies to be whelped. Some breeders add dried red raspberry leaves to the food a couple of weeks prior to whelping to counteract this problem. Your veterinarian can provide oxytocin or fast-absorbing calcium if the delivery is taking too long. Sometimes the last puppy or two—and these tend to be the largest—can be stillborn. If you have any doubts about retained puppies or placentas, consult with your veterinarian. Bitches usually eat all the placentas and they may have diarrhea afterward as a result. They will continue to pass a dark, brownish-red vaginal discharge for many days after whelping.

THE LITTER

The bitch will probably not want to leave her pups for the first twenty-four hours or so. Make sure she has access to fresh water. She likely won't eat much during that time. For the first week or two the bitch won't need as much food as she did just prior to whelping. But as the pups grow so will her appetite. Be prepared to pour on the feed, and make sure it is

Litter of ten-day-old Akbash pups. Photo by David Sims.

top-quality. Nursing bitches can eat four times their usual amount. If you are feeding a dry commercial food, supplement with yogurt, cottage cheese, eggs and meat.

Wherever she is nursing the pups, make sure the space is draft-free and warm, especially for the first two weeks. If you hear the pups making a lot of noise—a non-stop squeaking, mewling sound—there could be a problem. This can happen if they are too cold, too hot, sick or trapped

THE BIO-SENSOR METHOD

Researchers have suggested that mildly stressing young animals will stimulate development of their nervous systems. Benefits from such stimulation include improved cardiovascular performance, more efficient adrenal glands and greater resistance to stress and disease (Battaglia, 1995). Several exercises involving sensory stimulation can be performed on puppies from the age of three to eleven days. Termed the "Bio-Sensor Method," the steps are as follows:

1. Head pointed down: Hold the pup in both hands, belly side down, with head pointing toward the ground.
2. Supine position: Hold the pup in the palms of both hands so he is lying on his back, belly up. He may sleep, rest or even struggle in this position.
3. Tactile stimulation: Hold the pup in one hand and using a Q-tip, gently tickle him between any two toes on just one foot.
4. Thermal stimulation: Cool a damp towel in the refrigerator for five minutes, then place the pup on the towel, feet down. The pup is allowed to move at will.
5. Head held erect: Hold the pup in both hands with head pointing up, tail down, supporting the bottom of the pup.

Exercises can be done in any order and should only last three to five seconds each. Only perform them once each day. If a puppy resists, proceed carefully so as not to over-stress him. Pups can be overstimulated, so care should be taken not to traumatize them. However, the benefits of this gentle stimulation far outweigh any negative results.

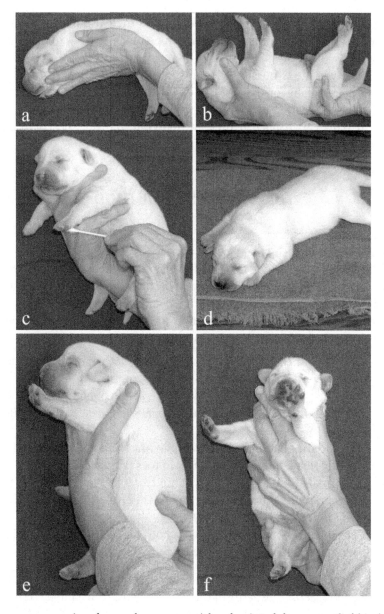

Bio-sensor exercises for newborn pups: a) head pointed down, pup held in both hands belly side down. b) supine position, pup lying on his back held in both hands. c) tactile stimulation, pup tickled between toes with a cotton swab. d) thermal stimulation, pup placed on cool, damp towel. e) and f) head held erect, pointing up, tail down, supported by both hands. Photos by Greg Lilley.

under their dam. Occasionally one strays away from the litter and mother isn't around or just hasn't managed to lead the pup back. We had a litter outside one year in the middle of a hot summer and found we had to mist them with water periodically to keep them cool enough so they would stop complaining. That may have been one time when a den in the earth would have been a good idea.

THE FIRST FEW WEEKS

Years ago conventional wisdom dictated that pups intended as livestock guardians should be left alone in the barn, not handled at all, and only exposed to the animals they were expected to live with. We now know that this type of rearing is a form of social isolation similar to pups being

Eighteen-day-old pups in a barn den lined with straw bales. A suspended log is indicated by the white arrow; this consists of a short piece of wood dangling by a rope or chain from the ceiling, placed such that it hangs just above the floor. This toy provides some stimulation in their otherwise bland environment. As the pups continue to mature and adjust to daily variations in temperature, further opportunities for exploration will be provided. Photo by David Sims.

raised in a kennel without human interaction or stimulation. We have seen a number of examples of adult dogs reared this way as pups—they are wild, barely manageable and sometimes dangerous. They are a liability on most modern farms and ranches. What we strive for today is to socialize our pups so they can be easily handled by people. Socialized pups will still bond to livestock. Dogs live in our world and depend on us to provide for them and to raise them so they can live successfully wherever we place them.

We also provide toys and obstacles in their pen to challenge and stimulate their brains from early on. When the pups are around four weeks of age, we encourage visitors, including well-behaved children, to come out and see them and to handle them gently. Further, we encourage

Early and continual socialization to people is important. This Alberta rancher makes frequent visits to check on the litter and spend time playing with and handling them. Photo by Irena Kneblewski.

At the same time the pups are also socialized to other species such as the horses and cats who share the barn. Photo by Irena Kneblewski.

new owners to expose their pups to all sorts of new things, like taking them on short rides, so that when changes occur later in their lives they will be better prepared and not traumatized.

Pups should be allowed to remain with their dams until they are seven to nine weeks of age. This is a critical time in their social development. During this time, they are learning bite inhibition from their littermates as they play. Their dam is also teaching them to respect her by growling and snapping at them when they get too rough. She will also give them signals when they can nurse or play with her. They are learning

Koza, an Akbash bitch has been sharing a fresh beef rib bone with her pup. Photo by Cindy Mellom.

Kangal pups learning how to play with and be respectful to their tolerant auntie, Sivas Regal Lule of Hakiki. Photo by Sue Kocher.

canine language, which will help them interact safely with other dogs once they have left the litter and gone into a new home. Removing pups much earlier can result in a dog with poor canine social skills.

MATCHING PUPPIES AND NEW OWNERS

We have included a questionnaire that breeders can use as a model to send to prospective owners. We suggest that breeders consider this

SAMPLE PLACEMENT QUESTIONNAIRE
PART I: LIVESTOCK GUARDIANS

Which type of livestock will the dog be guarding? ___ Sheep ___ Goats ___ Horses ___ Cattle ___ Poultry ___ Emu ___ Ostrich ___ Alpaca ___ Other _____

Will the dog also be a companion dog? ___ Children (Ages _____) ___ Adults ___ Elderly

Other companion animals in the home? ___ Dogs
(Which breeds, sexes, ages _____)
___ Cats ___ Birds ___ Others _____

Type and height of fencing and area enclosed _____
_____

Will the dog be with the stock or in a perimeter fence? Will the dog be only outside, or both inside and outside? _____
_____

Will there be a lot of visitors to your home/farm, or only occasional?
_____

Why do you want this particular breed instead of another livestock guardian breed? _____
_____

PART II: COMPANION DOGS/HOME GUARDIANS

Have you ever owned a large working breed of dog before? _____ Which breeds? _____

What other dogs have you owned/trained?_____
_____

What happened to any previous dogs? (Death by accident, disease, old age; got rid of because of behavior problems; left behind with family)
_____
_____

Do you currently have any other pets at home? _____ If so, what other species, breeds, sexes and ages? _____

Is anyone in your family allergic to dogs or other animals?_____

Does dog hair on clothing or furniture bother you? _____

Have you ever obedience-trained a dog before? _____ Is anyone in your family afraid of big dogs? _____ Who? _____

What do you think about crate-training? _____

Will the dog be alone during the day or night? _____

If the dog will be alone, what provisions do you plan to make, and where will the dog be kept?_____

Where will the dog sleep? _____

Who will the dog be a companion to? _____ Adults _____ Children
Ages_____

Who will be primarily responsible for the dog's care?_____

Who will train the dog (obedience classes?_____

Type and height of fencing and area enclosed_____
_____

In order to select a pup that is most compatible with you and your family, describe your own temperament and activities. Which activities do you expect to have your dog participate in? Use additional paper if necessary. _____
_____
_____

Why do you want a guard dog rather than just a companion dog like a Golden Retriever or Newfoundland dog?_____
_____

Why do you want an Livestock Protection Dog instead of another guard dog breed (such as German Shepherd Dog, Rottweiler)?
_____

Why do you want this particular breed instead of another livestock guardian breed ?
_____
_____

Which of the following temperaments do you prefer?
_____ Quiet/submissive _____ Steady/even-tempered _____ Lively/energetic
_____ Assertive/protective _____ Fierce/aggressive.

What expectations do you have of your dog?
_____
_____
_____
_____

Do you have nearby neighbors? _____

Do you know how they will feel about your owning a guard dog?_____

Are you aware of the laws governing dogs and owner responsibilities in your area, town? _____

Are you prepared to keep your dog indoors if he becomes a nuisance barker?_____

Do you have an obedience class in mind to take your dog to? _____

Are there puppy socialization classes in your area for pups three to six months? _____ (If you don't know, look into it. Early socialization classes are highly recommended for urban Livestock Protection Dogs.)

PART III: LIVESTOCK AND COMPANION DOG

Neutered dogs usually make better livestock guardians and companions. They guard just as well or better than intact dogs. Bitches in heat must be confined for three weeks every six to eight months and have been known to be irritable with both people and stock. Males can be distracted from their stock when a female is in season nearby, and can also be more irritable with people, stock, other dogs and pets. Dog breeding is time-consuming and provides little or no profit when done properly. Careful placement of pups is essential for successful integration with new families or livestock. Breeders should be able to raise and test their dogs with livestock in order to verify that those traits important in livestock protection are maintained. Dedicated and responsible breeders are welcome.

Do you plan to breed your dog if he/she qualifies as breeding quality?
No___ Maybe___ Yes___
Preferred coat length (if applicable): ___Long ___Medium ___Either
Sexual preference: ___Male ___Female ___Either
Any other traits you consider important for your dog to have?

_____

_____

part of the breeding and placement process as one of the most critical. Along with observing the behavior of the pups and testing them at about seven weeks of age, you will have to match the puppies with buyers. Sometimes matching will be difficult. Use your intuition if you have to, especially if you come across someone you are uncertain about. Be prepared to say you don't have the right pup for them—you may perhaps feel this person should be looking at another breed entirely, and not even in the livestock protection dog group. The decisions you make at this point will affect the lives of people, their livestock and that innocent puppy you are sending off. Being a breeder can be very difficult and stressful as you seek to match pups with buyers. Poor matches will come back to haunt you, guaranteed. If you don't think you're cut out for managing people as well as pups, perhaps you should reconsider breeding altogether. Successfully placing a litter takes a lot of skill, planning, and guts if you are going to do it right. If you get it wrong, you may end up with unhappy buyers, whose families or friends may have been injured by the dogs; miserable dogs; refunds; and worst of all, euthanized dogs that could have led meaningful, happy lives.

On the other hand, if you are successful at matchmaking, you will be receiving photos, letters, calls and e-mails praising your dogs, referrals from satisfied customers and solid new friends. Your bank account won't look much different, but you will know you're making a positive difference in lives and livelihoods out there. We have got it both right and wrong over the last twenty years—we lost a few dogs along the way, shed tears, pulled out handfuls of hair (mostly gray now). But we know our dogs have helped a lot of folks stay in business and have provided an abundance of love and comfort and protection to individuals and families. Perhaps best of all, some of our dearest friends came as a result of puppy placements.

CONCERNS FOR THE FUTURE

We sincerely hope that the decision to breed encompasses more than filling a market niche with saleable dogs. The breeds we've described in this book are the products of centuries of breeding choices made by people all over the world. Agriculturalists required and developed dogs that would protect their flocks and properties. The specialized traits that define livestock protection dogs are still prized by owners and breeders today, but are threatened when people breed for other purposes. The following comments from a Tibetan Mastiff owner echo the concerns of many breeders who are disturbed by a current trend in dog breeding— that of "dumbing down" the temperament and nature of our working breeds. This concern is particularly valid in view of sweeping anti-dog legislation around the world. She writes:

> What marks these large, wild, rustic creatures who came from the world of our ancestors is a certain independence of spirit, an ability to decide what is what without the interposition of human logic. Whether

people who are getting more and more into the groove of robotics can cope with the notion of something that will not merely do what it is told remains to be seen. If they cannot it will be a great pity, I feel, and a great light will have gone out of the world. I know, I know, old ladies say things like this. Likewise, they declare that the strawberries are not as sweet as when they were young. Could be.

Anyway, it is no joke coping with my two Tibetan Mastiff females, but I do it because something in them "calls" to me. It is the call that Rudyard Kipling described in his Jungle Book: "We are of one blood, thou and I." They bring me up against myself, and up against all that I have lost and continue to lose on those occasions when I merely go along without thinking things through for myself, or say "Yeah, whatever," when what I should say is, "This is an outrage which I will not put up with!"

Tolerant although they are, my second best is not nearly good enough for my dogs, and they quickly pull out of me things I didn't know I had left to give. They keep me on my toes. It isn't an easy life, and it isn't for everyone and was never meant to be. It is the life that my dogs have chosen for me, as I have chosen to take them into my life. I can never be thankful enough to them for what they have given, and I'd hate to see Tibetan Mastiff type dogs predominate the breed in years to come. I already have to put up with Chinese type food, kosher type restaurants, food look-alikes on airlines, and sterling silver plate in advertising.

In these rare breeds, we still have some semblance of a real thing. Real is worth keeping.   Mary Fischer, Flockguard E-List, 2002.

Another breeder accused a breed club of "trampling his democratic rights" to breed whatever and whenever he wanted, when a set of ethical guidelines for association-recognized breeders was suggested. Rather than investing in radiographs, pedigrees and unrelated bloodlines, he quit the club, established his own web site, and offered "perfect dogs for all needs" for sale. The rescue committee of the breed club spent the next five years dealing with the aftermath of this breeder's quick, easy sales. He eventually moved and gave no one his forwarding address.

The fact is that although there is a niche for more people-friendly, less aggressive dogs in more populated areas, we still have serious and deadly predators of livestock we have chosen to co-exist with. As long as this remains true, there will be a necessity for smart, tough livestock guardians.

THE CYCLE CONTINUES

Anyone with a bitch and stud can produce puppies. We appeal to each potential and current breeder to reach for the higher ground, to take a harder road. Remember what it was like when you first decided to get a pup or dog? What did you want from a breeder? Did your breeder take extra steps to make sure you had the best possible pup for your situation and your purposes? If she did not, what should she have done for you as a buyer? Would you go back to her for another dog, for advice? How do you want your puppy buyers to regard you? Now it is your turn to improve the quality and integrity of breeding.

In the end, you will reap what you sow. If you produce high quality pups with sound body and correct temperament, you will earn a fine reputation and you will always have new and repeat customers. If you compromise, your customers will not come back and, further, people will be warned away from you. You will not be rewarded financially or otherwise. One of the dearest wishes of conscientious breeders and owners everywhere is to put rescue services out of work. Please don't add to their burden.

As long as there are flocks to guard, there will be a place for livestock guardian dogs and ethical breeders. We expect the dogs to be with us for a long time. We hope this book helps all who wish to keep and champion these special breeds for many years to come.

Akbash mom shows pup that crates are places to relax and get away from it all. A good introduction before the scary plane ride. Photo by Diane Spisak.

Bibliography and Suggested Reading

The listings below include both sources that we have utilized during preparation of this book, and references that may prove useful to you for additional information. Several books may cover the same topic. We list all of them so that you will have a greater chance of finding one or two at your public library. Internet searches can also provide a number of useful websites, although be critical of any that are commercial and check out breeders thoroughly. If you plan to train a livestock protection dog as a companion on your own, we recommend that you read at least two training texts, completely, before beginning. Videotapes can also be very helpful for this purpose.

I. BREED INFORMATION

Ainsworth, Ivy. "Guarding the Kuvasz History." American Kennel Gazette 106 (4) (1989): 64-68.

Balsan, Francois. The Sheep and the Chevrolet: A Journey through Kurdistan. London, England: Paul Elek, 1947.

Black, Hal L. "Navajo Sheep and Goat Guarding Dogs: A New World Solution to the Coyote Problem." Rangelands 3 (1981): 235-37.

Black, Hal L. and Jeffrey S. Green. "Navajo Use of Mixed-Breed Dogs for Management of Predators." Journal of Range Management 38 (1985): 11-15.

Coppinger, Lorna and Ray Coppinger. "Livestock-Guarding Dogs that Wear Sheep's Clothing." Smithsonian 47 (1982): 64-73.

———. "So Firm a Friendship." Natural History 89 (1980): 12-26.

Coppinger, Ray and Lorna Coppinger. Dogs. New York: Scribner, 2001.

———. "Livestock-Guarding Dogs: An Old World Solution to an Age-Old Problem." Country Journal VII (1980): 68-77.

———. Livestock Guarding Dogs for U.S. Agriculture. Livestock Dog Project, MA: 1978.

Doherty, Brian. The Anatolian Karabash. Anatolian Karabash Club of Ireland. 7 Aberfoyle Terrace, Strand Road, Derry, N. Ireland, BT48-7NP, 1988.

Flamholtz, Cathy J. A Celebration of Rare Breeds. OTR Publications, 1986.

Follett-Orbegozo, Tamara. The Caucasian Ovcharka. Richville, NY: CVSI Press, 1996.

Green, Jeffrey S. and Roger A. Woodruff. "Breed Comparisons and Characteristics of Use of Livestock Guarding Dogs." Journal of Range Management (1988).

———. Guarding Dogs Protect Sheep from Predators. Agriculture Information Bulletin 588, Dubois, ID: USDA, 1990. An illustrated 31-page booklet, this is among the first training manuals published on the use of livestock guardian dogs, and reports the results of a survey on characteristics of a number of breeds being used in the early 1980s.

————. "The Use of Three Breeds of Dog to Protect Rangeland Sheep from Predators." Applied Animal Ethology 11 (1983/84): 141-61.

Gribble, Marilyn. The Hungarian Komondor. Middle Atlantic States Komondor Club, Inc., 1982. This interesting booklet and others can be purchased from the club secretary.

Hudak, L, C. Orkeny, I. Geczi, J. Hodosi and L. Vad. A Kuvasz. Edited by Jozsef Hodosi. Hungary: Hungaria Kuvasz Klub, 1996.

McGrew, John C. and Cindy S. Blakesley. "How Komondor Dogs Reduce Sheep Losses to Coyotes." Journal of Range Management 35 (1982): 693-96.

Morris, Desmond. Dogs—The Ultimate Dictionary of Over 1,000 Dog Breeds. North Pomfret, VT: Trafalgar Square Publishing, 2002.

Nelson, David D. & Judith N. Nelson. Akbash Dog—A Turkish Breed for Home and Agriculture. Akbash Dog Association, Int., Inc., 1983.

————. "The Livestock Guarding Dogs of Turkey." National Wool Grower 70 (1980): 12-14.

Rigg, Robin. Livestock Guarding Dogs: Their Current Use World Wide. IUCN/SSC Canid Specialist Group Occasional Paper No 1 (online): www.canids.org/occasionalpapers/

Rohrer, Ann and Cathy J. Flamholtz. The Tibetan Mastiff, Legendary Guardian of the Himalayas. OTR Publications, 1989.

Ryder, M. L. Sheep and Man. London, England: Gerald Duckworth and Co., 1983.

Sarkany, Pal and Imre Ocsag. Hungarian Dog Breeds. 2d ed. Budapest, Hungary: Corvina Press, 1987. This book may be purchased from the Middle Atlantic States Komondor Club. The breeds described in detail include Kuvasz and Komondor.

Schuler, Elizabeth Meriwether, ed. Simon and Schuster's Guide to Dogs. New York: Simon & Schuster, 1980.

Strang, Paul. The New Complete Great Pyrenees. New York: Howell Book House, 1991.

Walkowicz, Chris. Choosing a Dog for Dummies. New York: Hungry Minds, 2001.

Wilcox, Bonnie D.V.M. and Chris Walkowicz. The Atlas of Dog Breeds of the World. Neptune City, NJ: T.F.H. Publications, 1989. A huge book, 1,111 full color photos, 912 pages full of information on breeds more common and rare.

II. TRAINING

Bauman, Diane L. Beyond Basic Dog Training. New York: Howell Book House, 1987.

Benjamin, Carol Lea. Dog Problems. New York: Doubleday & Co., 1981. An excellent text for troubleshooting.

————. Dog Training for Kids. New York: Howell Book House, 1985.

————. Mother Knows Best—The Natural Way to Train Your Dog. New York: Howell Book House, 1986. Every dog owner should read this book. It is an easy-to-read, humorous, well-illustrated text about dogs, their behavior, their training, and the problems we create for them.

Bygrave, Lesley and Paul Dodd. Practical Training for Big Dogs. New York: Howell Book House, 1989.

Campbell, William E. Behavior Problems in Dogs. Goleta, CA: American Veterinary Publications, Inc., 1975. More clinical than the book by Benjamin, it is an excellent reference for professional trainers and serious dog enthusiasts.

————. A Guide to Better Behavior in Dogs. Loveland, CO: Alpine Publications, Inc., 1999. Another excellent text for raising a well-behaved companion dog.

Clothier, Suzanne. Body Posture and Emotions: Shifting Shapes, Shifting Minds. Stanton, NJ: Flying Dog Press, 1996. One of several fine booklets written by the author, this one on deciphering canine body language.

————. Finding a Balance: Issues of Power in the Human/Dog Relationship. Stanton, NJ: Flying Dog Press, 1996.

————. Understanding and Teaching Self Control. Stanton, NJ: Flying Dog Press, 1996.

Donaldson, Jean. The Culture Clash. Berkeley, CA: James & Kenneth, 1996. The author sheds light on a new understanding of the relationship between humans and domestic dogs.

————. Dogs Are from Neptune. Montreal: Lasar Multimedia Productions, Inc., 1998. The author provides candid answers to urgent questions about aggression and other aspects of dog behavior.

Dunbar, Ian. Sirius Puppy Training. New York: Bluford/Toth Productions, 1987. This is a videotape that demonstrates training techniques for young companion pups.

Evans, Job Michael. The Evans Guide for Counselling Dog Owners. New York: Howell Book House, 1985. As the title implies, this is not for beginners. The book is authoritative in its coverage of human-canine interactions, dealing mainly with the usual source of problems, the human.

Fisher, Betty and Suzanne Delzio. So Your Dog's Not Lassie—Tips for Training Difficult Dogs and Independent Breeds. New York: HarperCollins, 1998.

Fox, Michael W. Canine Behavior. Springfield IL: C. C. Thomas, 1965.

————. Understanding Your Dog. New York: Coward, McCann & Geoghegan, 1972.

Hart, Benjamin L. & Lynette A. Hart. Canine and Feline Behavioral Therapy. Philadelphia: Lea & Febiger, 1985.

Lorenz, Jay R. Introducing Livestock Guarding Dogs. Corvallis, OR: Oregon State University Extension Circular 1224, 1985.

Lorenz, Jay R. and Lorna Coppinger. How to Raise a Livestock Guard Dog. Corvallis, OR: Oregon State University Extension Circular 520, 1986.

Marlo, Shelby. New Art of Dog Training—Balancing Love and Discipline. Chicago: Contemporary Books, 1999.

McLennan, Bardi. Dogs and Kids—Parenting Tips. New York: Howell Book House, 1993.

Monks of New Skete. How to Be Your Dog's Best Friend: A training manual for dog owners. Boston/Toronto: Little-Brown & Co., 1978. Another classic, the Monks of New Skete do an excellent job of presenting the hows and whys of not just training a dog, but of understanding, appreciating and shaping your dog's behavioral attributes.

Pryor, Karen. 1985. Don't Shoot the Dog—The New Art of Teaching and Training. New York: Bantam Books, 1985. If training your dog in the basic commands has been enjoyable and you would like to learn more about the hows and whys of training techniques, here's a text for you. Other books we have referred to emphasize techniques specific to handling dogs. This book is unique and delightful in its analysis of training methods. Instead of telling you what to do with a dog, it tells you how and why we use training techniques.

Rugaas, Turid. Calming Signals: What Your Dog Tells You. Norway: Legacy by Mail, 2000. A forty-eight-minute video showing Rugaas at work.

———. On Talking Terms With Dogs: Calming Signals. Kula, HI: Legacy by Mail, Inc., 1997. A fascinating look at communication and how we can learn from dogs to help them overcome stress.

Rutherford, Clarice and David H. Neil. How to Raise a Puppy You Can Live With. Loveland, CO: Alpine Publications, 1999. Another fine classic.

Tortora, Daniel F. Understanding Electronic Dog-Training. Tucson, AZ: Tri-Tronics Inc., 1986. This is an informative instruction manual describing the use of electronic collars. It should be read prior to using any type of electronic collar.

Volhard, Joachim and Gail Tamases Fisher. Training Your Dog: The Step-by-Step Manual. New York: Howell Book House, 1983.

Vollmer, Peter J. SuperPuppy—How to Raise the Best Dog You'll Ever Have! Escondido, CA: SuperPuppy Press, 1988.

Wilson, Sylvia. Bite Busters: How to Deal with Dog Attacks. Australia: Simon & Schuster, 1997. An excellent little book on how to deal with dog attacks—what to look for in dog body language and how to react to safely escape injury.

III. HEALTH, NUTRITION, PUPPY APTITUDE TESTING, SELECTING A BREED AND GENERAL INTEREST

American Kennel Club. Canine Good Citizen Program—Participant's Handbook. Published by the A.K.C.

American Kennel Club. Gait, Observing Dogs in Motion. Videotape produced by the A.K.C.

Anderson, R.S., ed. Nutrition and Behavior in Dogs and Cats. New York: Proceedings of the First Nordic Symposium on Small Animal Veterinary Medicine (Oslo): Pergamon Press, 1982.

Bartlett, Melissa. "Follow-up: Puppy Aptitude Testing." Pure-Bred Dogs/American Kennel Gazette (May 1987): 64-71.

———. "A Novice Looks at Puppy Aptitude Testing." Pure-Bred Dogs/American Kennel Gazette (March 1979): 31-42.

———. "Puppy Aptitude Testing." Pure-Bred Dogs/American Kennel Gazette (March 1985): 31-34.

Battaglia, Dr. Carmen L. "Developing High Achievers." Pure-Bred Dogs/American Kennel Gazette (May 1995): 46-50.

Billinghurst, Ian B.V.Sc. The BARF Diet. Bathurst, Australia: Barfworld, 2001. Dr. Billinghurst describes a practical, commonsense way to feed raw diets to dogs for a long, healthy life. This diet is now called the BARF diet—biologically appropriate raw foods.

———. Give Your Dog a Bone. Bathurst, Australia: Dr. Ian Billinghurst, 1993.

———. Grow Your Pups with Bones. Bathurst, Australia: Dr. Ian Billinghurst, 1998.

Brinker, Wade. O., Donald L. Piermattei, and Gretchen L. Flo. Handbook of Small Animal Orthopedics and Fracture Treatment. Philadelphia: W. B. Saunders Co., 1983.

Bulanda, Susan. The Canine Source Book. 4th ed. Portland, OR: Doral, 1994. A catalogue of dog clubs, publications, organizations, associations, awards, contests, colleges of veterinary medicine and supply catalogues.

Childs, W. J. Across Asia Minor on Foot. London, 1917.

Clark, Ross D. and Joan R. Stainer, ed. Medical and Genetic Aspects of Purebred Dogs. Edwardsville, KS: Veterinary Medicine Publishing Co., 1983.

Clothier, Suzanne. Understanding Puppy Testing. Stanton, NJ: Flying Dog Press, 1996. An excellent overview and explanation of the entire process. Other behavior and training booklets available from Flying Dog Press: 1-800-735-9364 or www.flying dogpress.com.

Corley, E. A. Hip Dysplasia: A Monograph for Dog Breeders and Owners. Columbia MO: OFA Inc., University of Missouri-Columbia, 1983.

Duby, Georges. The Age of the Cathedrals: Art and Society 980–1420. Chicago: University of Chicago Press, 1981.

Elliot, Rachel Page. Dogsteps: A New Look. Doral Publishing, 2001. This is an excellent manual for those who wish to learn more about sound structure and how dogs move.

Elliot, Rachel Page. Dogsteps. A.K.C., 1988. This sixty-five-minute video provides an excellent discussion of dog structure and gait.

Fisher, G. T. and W. Volhard. "Puppy Personality Profile." Pure-Bred Dogs/American Kennel Gazette (March 1985): 36-42.

Giffin, James M.D. and Liisa Carlson, D.V.M. Dog Owner's Home Veterinary Handbook. 3rd ed. New York: Howell Book House, 1999. An excellent resource, 535 pages long, to keep on hand.

Gilbert, Edward M. Jr., and Thelma R. Brown. K-9 Structure and Terminology. New York: Howell Book House, 1995.

Goldstein, Martin, D.V.M. The Nature of Animal Healing. New York: Knopf, 1999.

Hastings, Pat and Bob Hastings. Puppy Puzzle: Evaluating Structural Quality. Dogfolk Enterprises, 1998. A fifty-five-minute videotape describing how to evaluate puppy structure to ensure you are getting a sound pup that will be able to perform his job and have the best chance of being a good breeding specimen.

Hodgson, Sarah. Puppies for Dummies. New York: Hungry Minds (IDG), 2000. Good reference for selecting and training a companion pup.

Kerns, Nancy. "Choose the Best Dry Food." The Whole Dog Journal (February 2002): 3-7. An excellent holistic journal containing no paid advertising.

Kilcommons, Brian and Sarah Wilson. Paws to Consider—Choosing the Right Dog for You and Your Family. New York: Warner Books, 1999.

Lanting, F. L. Canine Hip Dysplasia and Other Orthopedic Problems. Loveland, CO: Alpine Publications, 1980.

Lowell, Michele. Your Purebred Puppy—A Buyer's Guide. New York: Henry Holt & Co., 1990. A down-to-earth, practical guide for choosing a breed and a puppy. It does not cover many rare breeds, but gives factual information about those it does.

McGinnis, Terri. The Well Dog Book. New York: Random House Inc., 1974.

Pitcairn, Richard H. and Susan Hubble Pitcairn. Dr. Pitcairn's Complete Guide to Natural Health for Dogs and Cats. Emmaus, PA: Rodale Press, Inc., 1995. Holistic medicine made practical.

Shook, Larry. The Puppy Report. New York: Lyons and Burford, 1992. This investigative reporter describes how reckless breeding threatens to ruin purebred dogs...and how a healthy puppy can be yours.

Volhard, Wendy and Kerry Brown, D.V.M. The Holistic Guide for a Healthy Dog. New York: Howell Book House, 1995. Includes raw food, natural diet recipes.

Walkowicz, Chris. Choosing a Dog for Dummies. New York: Hungry Minds (IDG), 2001. A good basic reference for selecting the right breed and puppy.

Wulff-Tilford, Mary L. and Gregory L. Tilford. All You Ever Wanted to Know About Herbs for Pets. Irvine, CA: BowTie Press, 1999.

IV. MAGAZINES

American Kennel Gazette (A.K.C.): www.akc.org

Bloodlines (U.K.C.): www.ukcdogs.com/pb/bloodlines.html

Dogs in Canada (C.K.C.): www.dogs-in-canada.com

Dog Fancy: www.animalnetwork.com/dogfancy

Dog World: www.dogworldmag.com

Off Lead: www.offlead.com, 717-691-3388

The Whole Dog Journal: www.whole-dog-journal.com, 800-424-7887

V. WEBSITES

www.AVAR.org Association of Veterinarians for Animal Rights. Guide to congenital and heritable disorders in dogs; includes genetic predisposition to diseases for 152 breeds, and lists genetically transmitted diseases.

www.caninesports.com Dr. Chris Zink, an expert in canine sports medicine, provides some interesting and practical tips on keeping dogs fit and healthy.

www.flockguard.org Described as livestock and family guardian dog comprehensive resource gateway.

www.flyingdogpress.com Suzanne Clothier's Flying Dog Press. Source of articles online as well as ordering information for her excellent booklets on training and understanding dogs and their relationships to people.

www.kuvaszclubofcanada.org/steve A thorough description of all aspects of the Kuvasz.

www.lgd.org Livestock Guardian Dog Association. A variety of articles and links for many breeds and groups.

www.offa.org The Orthopedic Foundation for Animals database for canine hip dysplasia and other orthopedic diseases, as well as thyroid and cardiac disorders.

www.workingdogs.com/genetics.htm Web resources for canine genetics.

www.upei.ca/~cidd Canine Inherited Disorders Database, out of University of Prince Edward Island.

www.vet.upenn.edu/research/centers/pennhip PennHip procedures explained for the evaluation and certification of dogs for hip dysplasia.

Livestock Protection Dog Breed Associations and Other Contacts

The breed association and rescue addresses listed below include contacts who were willing to be listed. The names and addresses were current at the time of publication. Most breed clubs and many breeders have websites, so if you cannot find what you are looking for, we recommend an internet search.

Akbash Dogs International (ADI)
Orysia Dawydiak, Registrar
1666 Union Rd, R.R. 3
Charlottetown, PE C1A 7J7 Canada
(902) 672-3036
www.whitelands.com/akbash

Alentejo Shepherd Dog Club of Portugal
Clube Português do Rafeiro do Alentejo
Rua Augusto Eduardo Nunes, 12
7000-651 Évora, Portugal

Alentejo Shepherd Dog Breeders' Association
Associação dos Criadores do Rafeiro do Alentejo
Apartado 34
7450-999 Monforte, Portugal
Tel: + 351 245 573 620 / + 351 962 604 059
Fax: + 351 245 573 423
acra@portugalmail.pt
www.alentejodigital.pt/acra

American Kuvasz Association (AKA)
Linda Munson
P.O. Box 121016
New Brighton, MN 55112 USA
Vizard-Kuvasz@juno.com
www.kuvasz.org

American Tibetan Mastiff Association (ATMA)
Martha Feltenstein, President
35 West 23rd St, 3rd Floor
New York, NY 10010 USA
(212) 620-7663
zuleika371@aol.com
www.tibetanmastiff.org

Anatolian Shepherd Dogs International, Inc. (ASDI)
P.O. Box 429
Busnell, FL 33513 USA
ballester@anatolianshepherd.cc
shabazin@aol.com
http://anatoliandog.org

Anatolian Shepherds' Dogs Worldwide, Inc. (ASDW)
Beth Goldowitz, USA
(308) 485-4105
asdwinc@aol.com
www.anatolianshepherd.com

Anatolian Shepherd Dog Club of America, Inc. (ASDCA)
845 Chariot Trail
Limestone, TN 37681 USA
(715) 443-3509
www.asdca.org

Castro Laboreiro Watch Dog Club
Clube do Cão de Castro Laboreiro
Apartado 76
2544-909 Bombarral, Portugal
Tel: + 351 938 616 010
Fax: + 351 262 603 288
c_laboreiro@hotmail.com
http://planeta.clix.pt/cccl

Caucasian Ovcharka (Mountain Dog) Club of America (COCA)
P.O. Box 227
Chardon, OH 44024 USA
(440) 286-2374
cocaclub@aol.com
www.cocaclub.us

Estrela Mountain Dog Association of Portugal
Associação Portuguesa do Cão da Serra da Estrela
Estrada Nacional, 37
Boavista
2560-426 Silveira, Portugal
Tel: + 351 261 933 278
 Fax: + 351 261 933 278
apcse@iol.pt

Estrela Mountain Dog Breeders and Friends League
Liga dos Criadores e Amigos do Cão da Serra da Estrela
Av. 1° de Maio (Club Camões)

6290-541 Gouvia, Portugal
Tel: + 351 238 492 747

Great Pyrenees Club of America (GPCA)
Catherine de la Cruz, Livestock Guardian Chair
4445 B Gravenstein Hwy
Sebastopol, CA 95472-6001 USA
(707) 829-1655
cdlcruz@sonic.net
http://clubs.akc.org.gpca/

Great Pyrenees Club of Central Ontario (GPCCO)
Norma Egginton
Prestonfield Farm
R.R. 5
Rockwood, ON N0B 2K0 Canada
(519) 856-9267
Fax: (519) 853-9355

Kangal Dog Club of America (KDCA)
Sue Kocher, USA
admin@kangalclub.com
www.kangalclub.com
www.ukcdogs.com/GuardianDogs/KangalDog.std.htm

Komondor Club of America (KCA)
http://clubs.akc.org/kca/ (USA)

Kuvasz Club of Canada (KCC)
Steve Hounsell, President
2057 Harvest Dr.
Mississauga, ON L4Y 1T7 Canada
(905) 276-4462
steve.hounsell@rogers.com
www.kuvaszclubofcanada.org

Kuvasz Fanciers of America, Inc. (KFA)
Tom Lukaszczyk, President
P.O. Box 80596
Bakersfield, CA 93380 USA
(661) 587-8141
lukas-kuvasz@att.net
http://members.aol.com/kfa4kuvasz

Maremma Sheepdog Club of America (MSCA)
Mary Jarvis, Secretary-Treasurer
2868 S Peterson Rd

Poplar, WI 54864 USA
(715) 364-2646
grovland@discover-net.net
www.all-animals.com/maremma

Middle Atlantic States Komondor Club (MASKC)
Joy Levy, Corresponding Secretary
102 Russel Road
Princeton, NJ 08540 USA
(609) 924-0199
www.komondor.com/maskc/

Polish Tatra Sheepdog Club of America (PTSCA)
Carol Wood
P.O. Box 2183
Florence, OR 97439 USA
awftatra@oregonfast.net
Diana Rymarz, USA
adrymarz@aol.com
www.ptsca.com/

Pyrenean Mastiff Club of America (PMCA)
Karin S. Graefe
24307 Magic Mountain Pkwy, Ste 338
Santa Clarita, CA 91355
(661) 724-0268
dogs@qnet.com
www.pyreneanmastiff.org

United States Tibetan Mastiff Club (USTMC)
www.ustmc.com (USA)

U.S. Caucasian Ovcharka Preservation Society (USCOPS)
ovcharka@aol.com
www.ovcharka-breeds.com
Yugoslavian Sarplaninac
www.ukcdogs.com/GuardianDogs/Sarplaninac.std.htm

Organizations working with multiple breeds:
Grupo Lobo - Associação Para a Conservação do Lobo e do Seu Ecossitema
(Wolf Group—Association for the conservation of the wolf and its ecosystem)
Faculdade de Ciências da Universidade de Lisboa, Ed.
Departamento de Zoologia e Antropologia, Bloco C2, 3° Piso
Campo Grande
1749-016 Lisboa, Portugal
Tel: + 351 217 500 073
Fax: + 351 217 500 028
globo@fc.ul.pt

Carla Cruz
Portuguese LGD Breeds
Pta. Manica, n°6-3° Dto.
2780-022 Oeiras, Portugal
+ 351 96 296007
carla_cruz@oninet.pt
lgdport@hotmail.com

Livestock Guard Dog Association
Lorna and Ray Coppinger
Hampshire College
Amherst, MA 01002 USA
(413) 549-4600, ext. 348
lcfc@hamp.hampshire.edu

Roger Woodruff, USDA
APHIS Wildlife Services
720 O'Leary Street, NW
Olympia, WA 98502 USA
(360) 753-9884

Jeffrey S. Green, USDA
APHIS Wildlife Services
2150 Centre Ave, Bldg B
Mail Stop 3W9
Ft. Collins, CO 80526-8117 USA
(970) 494-7453

Robin Rigg
Slovak Wildlife Society
Flat 5, 4 Chatsworth Road
NW2 4BN, Kilburn, London, UK
Tel: + 44-(0)208-4517555
info@slovakwildlife.org.uk
www.slovakwildlife.org.uk

The American Kennel Club (A.K.C.)
260 Madison Ave.
New York, NY 10016 USA
(212)696-8200
www.akc.org

The Canadian Kennel Club (C.K.C.)
89 Skyway Ave, Suite 100
Etobicoke, ON M9W 6R4 Canada
(800)250-8040 or (416)675-5511
www.ckc.ca

The United Kennel Club (U.K.C.)
100 E Kilgore Rd
Kalamazoo, MI 49002-5584 USA
(616)343-9020
www.ukcdogs.com

Rescue Organizations:
Some rescue individuals and groups are affiliated with specific breeds and breed clubs, while others work with multiple breeds and crosses. Some groups specialize in companion dogs; others will place dogs in working situations. When known and provided, the state, province, country and club affiliation are listed next to names.

Akbash Dogs
Pat Wolter, (AZ) (ADI)
(602) 569-9448
pwolter@cox.net

Diane Spisak (KS) (ADI)
(785) 883-4774
spisak@grapevine.net

Sunny Reuter (ON) (ADI)
(905) 884-7924
sammyarko@hotmail.com

Anatolian Shepherd Dogs
National Anatolian Shepherd Rescue Network
www.petfinder.org/shelters/AZ41.html
www.nationalanatolianshepherdrescuenetwork.com
www.nasrn.org

Carleen Conyers
ResQRanger@webtv.net
NASRN@nasrn.org
(480) 899-1341
Fax: (413) 460-6623
www.goatworld.com/rescue.shtml
http://community.webtv.net/ResQRanger/ANATOLIANSHEPHERD

Karen Massa
rkma@juno.com

Anatolian Shepherd Dogs International
www.anatoliandog.org/rescue.htm

Caucasian Ovcharka
Audrey Chalfen
caucasus@aol.com

Benjamin G. Levy
ben-levy@westworld.com
www.westworld.com/~ben-levy/rescue.html

Caucasian Ovcharka Club of America
www.ovcharkarescue.org

Great Pyrenees

Debi Carpadus (CA) (GPCA)
(916) 452-7977
Great Pyrenees Rescue of Northern California, Inc.
rescue@gprnc.org
www.gprnc.org

Cindy Barch (IL) (GPCA)
(309) 827-6143
clbarch@attglobal.net

Kathleen Appleton (IL) (GPCA)
(847) 668-7297
WhiteGentleGiants@yahoo.com

Martha Rehmeyer (NC) (GPCA)
(336) 768-4142
luvmypyrs@triad.rr.com

Mitzi Potter (OK)
(405) 260-0845
mitzi@mitzis.net

Greta Osterman (PA) (GPCA)
(610) 346-9552
gretaost@aol.com

Barb Bowes (PA) (GPCA)
(732) 892-0360
bamb@monmouth.com

Tara Morrison (MN) (GPCA)
(651) 653-4537
monterrapyrs@yahoo.com
www.members.tripod.com/northstar_pyr

Carol Graham (ON) (GPCCO)
(519) 853-3005

Norma Egginton (ON) (GPCCO)
(519) 856-9267
Fax (519) 856-9355

Arlene Griffin-Van Dallen (PQ)
(450) 424-4019
grifvan@sprint.ca

Judy McPherson (ON—Ottawa region)
(613) 673-5837
cairns.clydes@cyberus.ca

Kangal Dog
Lorie Jordan (OH) (KDCA)
(330) 821-6968
xena55s6@aol.com

Sue Kocher (NC)
(919) 870-0050
skocher@mindspring.com

Komondor
Sandy Hanson (WI) (KCA)
(262) 594-3374

Kuvasz
Mary Brownell (VT)
(802) 442-8693
brownll@sover.net

Cindy Pearce (NJ)
kuvaszmom@aol.com

Gail S. Dash (CA)
kuvasz@pacbell.net
kuvaszresq@aol.com

Robert Nierstheimer (VA, DC, NC, WV)
kuvasz@cox.net
rescue@kuvasznet.com

Geral Triplett (KY) - working dogs
(859) 879-3750
kuvasz@gte.net

Dan Wasson (MI) (AKA)
BlitzKuvas@aol.com

Ivonne Lukaszczyk (CA) (KFA)
(661) 587-8141
lukas-kuvasz@att.net

American Kuvasz Association
www.kuvaszok.org/kuvrescue.htm
rescue@kuvasz.org

Kuvasz Fanciers of America
http://members.aol.com/kfa4kuvasz/
    rescue.htm

Jan & Olga Schmidt (ON) (KCC)
(519) 443-7088
brntwood@execulink.com

Maremma Sheepdog
Laura Steenburg (IL)
(847) 713-2043
LBSteenburg@aol.com

Mary Jarvis (WI) (MSDA)
grovland@discover-net.net

Polish Tatra
Diana Rymarz (MS) (PTSCA)
(601) 849-9477
adrymarz@aol.com

Sara Wojciechowski (OH) (PTSCA)
(513) 521-9472
wojo@fuse.com

Carol Wood and Dr. Turner Wood
    (OR) (PTSCA)
(541) 902-8740
awftatra@oregonfast.net

Pyrenean Mastiff
Karin S. Graefe (CA) (PMCA)
(661) 724-0268
dogs@qnet.com

Tibetan Mastiff
American Tibetan Mastiff Association
info@tibetanmastiff.org

The authors request that you contact them with any comments,
questions, and that you share your unusual experiences with livestock
protection dogs for future editions of this book. They can be reached at:

Orysia Dawdyiak - dawydiak@upei.ca

David E. Sims - sims@upei.ca
Department of Biomedical Sciences
Atlantic Veterinary College
University of Prince Edward Island
550 University Avenue
Charlottetown, Prince Edward Island
Canada C1A 4P3

Made in the USA
Middletown, DE
05 July 2021